T0339427

Speaking Up in a Culture of Silence

We know we should speak up and question what is being taken as normal in our work cultures – to notice and call out bad behaviour and resist being silenced. This book is a guide to what it takes to do this in a way that doesn't expose you to the countermeasures of people who do not like being questioned. What is explored through case studies and personal experience are ideas about how to resist being silenced at work where there are competing demands on your time and energy and where people have learnt to tolerate bad and uncivil behaviours just to get the work done. There are no magic solutions or calls for decisive action. Just some modest ideas about what can help you hold onto your voice and your thinking so that when the time is right, you can say something that just may help keep us all a bit safer.

Speaking Up in a Culture of Silence

Changing the Organization Activity from Bullying and Incivility to One of Listening and Productivity

Dr. David Naylor

Routledge
Taylor & Francis Group

A PRODUCTIVITY PRESS BOOK

Cover and text illustrations by Jo Compton

First published 2023
by Routledge
605 Third Avenue, New York, NY 10158

and by Routledge
2 Park Square, Milton Park, Abingdon, Oxon, OX14 4RN

*Routledge is an imprint of the Taylor & Francis Group,
an informa business*

Library of Congress Cataloging-in-Publication Data
A catalog record for this title has been requested

ISBN: 978-1-032-29846-7 (hbk)
ISBN: 978-1-032-29845-0 (pbk)
ISBN: 978-1-003-30232-2 (ebk)

DOI: 10.4324/9781003302322

Typeset in ITC Garamond
by Apex CoVantage, LLC

Contents

Preface

This book emerged out of failure. I was trying to help a team explore why bullying and incivility had become embedded in their work culture, why their people survey indicated a trend that some people found this work culture difficult – long work hours, some shouting and swearing; intrusion into home life with late-night texts requiring action – but also a culture that pushed people to their best work and a sense of achievement, which propelled their careers forward.

I spent a lot of time listening to clever, highly motivated people, trying to understand what they were feeling, why that was and what they would like to be different. I worried about some of them. A few seemed to be edging towards not being able to cope and assuming that this state of affairs was in some way their fault. It was as if this personal distress was the price some had to pay to silence a conversation about why work was organised in such a way as to make it necessary to shout and swear to get things done. To use people up. Good and capable people. People who were expensive to employ and to recruit. People who came to believe they were not good enough. I decided I wanted to have a go at developing an approach that offered a bit more hope. Some practical action that was more than a poster on the wall about being nice and calling out bad behaviour.

Of course, it was not as simple as this. I was angry with the senior team for allowing this culture to develop. A feeling that only diminished when I finally and reluctantly thought about my own behaviour in leadership roles. I was not without sin. I had been and remained capable of being indifferent, uncaring and unkind. I could be that person shouting, demanding to have it my way. With the kindness[1] of good colleagues, I came to see that this should not stop me from trying to write about what I knew. I just had to do it in a way that let readers know that I didn't think there was a small group of people who made other people's lives difficult and that this sort of behaviour had nothing to do with me. What helped me think about the ideas in this book was joining the dots of my own experience.

Like lots of other people I had experienced being silenced and being advised to forget things and get back to normal. A phrase I hate for its silencing intention. My situation was the sudden death of my brother when I was 18. Not a unique experience but it might as well have been for all the help we got. It was an event best managed by not talking about it.

Something to be kept private. Eventually, I met people who were prepared to sit and listen and this in some ways was the beginning of my inquiry into what silences us and what we can do to resist this.

Back in 2008 I researched the skills required to be 'constructively awkward' for my doctorate while working at The King's Fund in London. I got to talk to people who refused to be quiet; who found a way to question explanations about why people were underachieving in school or subject to the disempowering racist indifference of some of our institutions. Modest people who asked good questions. Who could think on their feet and talked in ways that sustained and built relationships. Any idiot can shout that everyone else is wrong and believe that thinking they are right is the same as being right. That person's silence is evidence of their agreement. It takes skill and kindness to create the conditions for a conversation about what is really going on here, when people are attached to their worldview and events are unfolding as you talk. To have this conversation on the street, in an ordinary room, on an ordinary Wednesday afternoon. A conversation where there is no hiding behind technology or anonymous social media posts. The person I spoke to took risks. They accepted they could get it wrong. That some people would pile in at the slightest mis-step. They were people who valued conversation over anything else. They believed in argument, the exchange of ideas, a curiosity about other people's values and beliefs and trying to do good.

These are people, who in the words of Tom Wolfe,[2] had the 'right stuff'. Who had a combination of courage and skill and unlike the people he was describing were also ordinary. They didn't act the hero and they helped me understand that more becomes possible if you stop holding yourself to an impossible standard. That we need to notice and then resist the spiral down into imaginary interventions and brilliant comebacks that are never spoken. To not be the hero is to stay connected to what is possible, given the context. This was the next lesson. Context is nearly everything. To notice who else is present, what they are doing, the task in hand, or if people have eaten recently or are so tired, a biscuit and a cup of tea is the best intervention you can offer right now.

If I notice who else is present, I can step back from another aspect of the hero. My imaginary heroic self is always a loner. I look in. I do not look out. People who are serious in their resistance to being silenced, who are capable of being constructively awkward tend to notice and want to work with others. This means we can think of speaking up as a team effort. Think this and you bring others into view. In particular the bystander.

If I am not being silenced; if I am not the one doing the silencing; then I am a bystander. A role that is associated with passivity; the turning of a blind eye and deaf ear. It can be so. It is also a role with the potential to make speaking up, going against the grain, safer for whoever takes the lead. Imagine you have gathered the courage to speak in what feels to you a hostile environment. You can no longer stand by; your values are being ignored by your inaction. As you finish speaking, as your heart rate remains high, as you anticipate that awful silence, you hear a voice—*I think we should listen to (your name here), let's take a moment, have a think and talk it through; maybe we are missing something here. Thanks (your name here).* Imagine if that is your boss talking, who sees her job as creating a sense of sufficient safety for people to talk. She does not assume such attention to how speaking happens in her team or department in any way undermines her authority to also say—*just do this, please.*

This is a book for busy people, who do not have the time to read every page. I have used lots of case material to argue for a different way of thinking about the behaviours that can silence people and wreck job satisfaction and productivity. Each chapter explores a different theme. If you are on the receiving end of bullying behaviour or a witness to it read Chapter 2. If you have been silenced by your boss or are interested in how to help a colleague in distress, when you only have a few minutes, start with Chapter 3. If you are interested in how to be constructively awkward have a look at Chapters 4 and 6. If you are leading a team, department or organisation and want to investigate why people keep saying, via the staff survey, that they feel unsafe, read Chapter 5 and be prepared to think about your leadership. If you are facing a troubling moment and worry about going quiet, explore the ideas in Chapter 7. Finally, if hope has gone and silence is the only option for now, read Chapter 8.

As you read remember that this is not about heroic action. No 'going over the top' or 'heads above the parapet'. What I describe here is an approach anchored in the assumption that speaking up is not a superpower. It is a fluctuating skill, best exercised with the help of others. That in the end if we choose to be quiet, we can choose to stay present; thinking about what is going on; thinking about what matters to us as we wait for a safer moment to speak.

Notes

1 Do not mistake kindness for soft and nice or agreement. Kindness is tough; it is giving the time, attention and your best thinking to a situation.
2 Wolfe, T. (2005) *The right stuff.* London: Vantage.

About the author

David Naylor, DProf, MA, is a director of a consultancy practice researching and developing practical interventions to mitigate the effects of bullying and incivility for individuals, teams and services. Previously, he worked as a senior consultant at The King's Fund. He has a professional doctorate and a MA in organisational change. He trained in consultancy at the Tavistock, facilitation at the University of Surrey and has a diploma in psychodynamic counselling from Birkbeck.

Chapter 1

Introduction

In most meetings, pride or caution still forbid one to say what one feels most deeply. The noise of the world is made out of silences.[1]

DOI: 10.4324/9781003302322-1

It's the second module of an aspiring leader's programme. I am standing in front of a group of people who are at the top of their game clinically and find themselves invited to take up a leadership role they have had little training for. We are talking about facilitating meetings and how you help people engage and talk. James, a surgeon, begins to talk about the pressure he can be under to improvise, when the right equipment is not available. He is at pains to point out that while it's safe, it's not as safe as it should be. The problem is that his boss does not want to hear his concerns. What should he do?

I have no idea what he should do, and I think I should know. I notice myself leaving the room, while my body stays in front of the group. This is me, fleeing the scene and my sense of incompetence. I notice that thinking has become difficult and my mouth is dry. I decide that saying something is better than this silence. This is usually a mistake. 'You need to confront him', I say. I know, and he knows, this is useless advice, uttered by me to escape the moment. That this neatly replicates when he and his boss tacitly agree not to explore the issue of correct instruments.

This was an event I think about often. Some good came of it. I decided I would research the topic of speaking up. Talk to people who had a reputation for being constructively awkward. To build a practical theory, so next time I was asked what to do, I could offer some useful ideas. However, what remained hidden to me was the link I had made between speaking up and being heroic; I believed that calling ideas and people out was the work of a brave few. People who had the right stuff. Underneath, I believed I should learn from them, but I would never be quite them. I would forever compare myself unfavourably to the imaginary person I should be. As such, I missed some of what I was capable of.

This comparison was a consequence of my own upbringing; as an English, white, male, second child of middle-class parents, who had grown up during the 1930s. It was the process by which I was inducted into the world of conversation and power. A process we all go through, regardless of background. I learnt about who I should speak to, about what, when, with what tone and language. An education renewed each time I joined a new group, profession, or organisation. There were always rules and rituals to learn. If I wanted to belong, I had better follow them. I learnt to be circumspect in my questioning, to go along with what was accepted as normal around here. The part of me that knew I should challenge, and question was hived off into some imaginary person I rarely was.

On that day with the surgeon, I came face to face with this gap. The gap between what I was capable of, if I took the time to think, and what I imagined I was capable of—as that imaginary heroic figure in my head. When I spoke from this imaginary place my advice was vacuous. When I took my time to think, wait and practise, I was capable of questioning and challenge. I could go against the grain, but it would always be modest—the action of someone ordinary, not heroic.

Taking up the path of the ordinary means I gave up the idea I would speak every time I need to and want to. Accepting this has (mostly) freed me from the sense of failure that has dogged my thinking about this subject. If I stop imagining there is some heroic part of me, who already knows how to be straight talking, I can face an interesting question:

What is being asked of me in this situation?

This is not my question. It is the work of Andrew McKie.[2] He explored the ethical duty of nurses to resist leadership that would do harm; in a historical context of complicity and the failure to say no. I read it as a reminder that I need to be vigilant. My silence can be taken as my tacit support of leadership, good and bad. It is also a powerful question in relation to this book. How do I remain alert to my duty to think and act, when I can, and what can help me do this?

When I ask this question, I am agreeing with myself, that I maybe need to stop and think about what I am seeing and hearing as I sit here in this meeting or conversation. It is the first step in building the sense of purpose or agency I will require if I decide to intervene. It is a question that poses another relevant question:

> *What sort of team, department, division or organisation am I a part of?*

This question widens the scope of my thinking. The decision to speak (or not) is usually framed as a personal choice: a choice emergent from a complex, hard-to-understand intrapsychic process. While it is, this is to simplify the task of speaking up. It overemphasises personal responsibility that is neither fair nor helpful. Telling people to speak up, say more, be candid is useless advice without posing the second question. This question brings into critical view the context we find ourselves in. That is, the people around us; our professional roles and know-how; our task; and our conversational culture. These factors help determine what happens as I face the question—what is being asked of me?

If we can bring context into view to understand how others are thinking and behaving, and how this adds up to how we talk to each other around here, we can ask a third question:

> *What can I do to help others speak and resist being silenced?*

The assumption threaded through the chapters in this book is that speaking up is best done with others. This means thinking about the four 'positions' we can occupy in a team meeting or difficult conversation that unfolds in the weekly division meeting. We can be the speaker; we can be the intended recipient of what is said; we can be bystanders to this exchange; and we can be one of the people (often in senior roles) who have created the wider organisational context of our conversation.

The purpose of the book is to explore the three questions; to be a guide for people who want to understand why it can be so hard to speak up in our organisations and teams. People who want, when required, to be 'constructively awkward' to 'go against the grain' at work. To question what is assumed to be the right and correct ways of thinking and behaving around here. Where the pressures to stay quiet are real and an exhortation to speak up and be candid feels inadequate in the face of real and imagined intimidation. Where policies about a duty of candour can reinforce a sense of personal failure. Policies based on an inadequate understanding of how silence and silencing works in the daily life of our organisations.

This is for people who want more to be said in their meetings and conversations. Who wonder what they can do differently to enable this. For senior people, who, as they walk into the room, notice the conversation changes. Where people choose their words carefully, edit the data; avoid overt conflict; and where silence is taken as agreement. The sort of meeting people leave, then talk elsewhere about what[3] they think, know and feel. The sort of conversation that, if it could be had at the time, would perhaps keep us all a bit safer.

This is for those who can be the ones exerting the pressure to silence others. Who use their power in coercive ways and feel trapped in an enforcer role. For people who find themselves trying to simplify or suppress the intractable dilemmas that shape complex work.

Finally, this is for anyone who thinks the suppression of alternative views and dissenting voices. Who, like me, given the right context, can occupy the role of silencer; silenced; and bystander.

Working in the gap

About a week before the deadline for the first draft of the book, I got a call. It was from a senior manager who said they had a problem with bullying. A few of their most experienced people were making life difficult for the local management team. They needed someone to come in and sort things out. As she spoke, we both realised that what she wanted most was a safe enough place to talk it through. She had been holding this feud for a while and had had enough. She knew that whatever was going on was not being 'worked'. She was good at being patient and not getting cross. Other people saw that and left her to it. She wanted to try and change that perception and get people talking.

We agreed that this would be interesting and hard work. No surprise she wanted to get someone in. If we had been speaking a couple of years ago, I would have volunteered. Hard to pass up an opportunity to test ideas and feel clever. Luckily a similar invitation, which I had accepted, had not gone well. Stepping into other people's teams or organisations is not as helpful as people already working there taking up an inquiry or intermediary role.

Intermediaries are people who can navigate between organisational structures and cultures. People who want to bring sides together for mutual learning; who reject the idea of winning and losing and the silencing of dissenting voices. People who may intimately know the destructive power of being silenced. People who, despite this experience, are kind and direct; not prone to hubris; who accept that organisational life is mostly messy. People who assume complex situations require a both/and approach; who know that even if they lack positional power, there are ways to dislodge the certain. People who embrace the 'way of the weak'.[4] The determination to modify relationships between people, even the powerful, by carefully considering how they think, speak and behave. Work that requires patience, and the ability to cope with one's fear.

Coming back to the call with the senior manager.

We talked about the information that may be useful to offer people who can behave badly. Sometimes such people do not understand the impact of their behaviour, particularly if their own professional education involved similar treatment. I advised that the evidence is clear: bullying and incivility negatively impact our thinking and willingness to collaborate. Being told to shut the **** up silences the recipient and those who are bystanders. Everyone ends up thinking a bit less and becomes preoccupied with trying to explain why we are being treated badly; or plotting revenge; or thinking about finding another job. We agreed this team was expensive, so it was odd there was such tolerance of this attack on that precious commodity—people's thinking and know-how. If someone was stealing the photocopier or intellectual property, senior people would be involved. But this loss was accepted.

I said the people behaving badly probably knew it was unhelpful. Simply telling people to stop, be nice, speak up, does not usually work. These behaviours are entrenched in our organisations and teams. It is how some work gets done. The problem is that our explanations for its presence are insufficient, leading to weak interventions. My choice of language triggered a short conversation about getting HR in and dealing with the culprits in a 'tough and robust manner'. It is tempting to retaliate but we decided on another course of action, which in the end may be much tougher on the people involved. It was to get people to stop and pause for a sufficient time to think about how their behaviour might be clues about something problematic in the team and wider system. The consequence of unprofessional behaviour is twofold. The harm it does to individuals; and the hidden harm through the silencing of inquiring and dissenting voices; leading to unsafe, narrow and inefficient ways of working.

She decided she would work with a colleague and as they went about the everyday meetings notice when things 'kicked off'. Paying attention to who was in the room; the topic of conversation; and what people did as things developed. To try and build an understanding of what the underlying cause may be that leads a few clever, apparently sane people, to behave like this and why others sat around and said nothing. She was trying to get some grip on a dimension of her service that was really hard to talk about—the conversational culture.

How people talk to each other, who gets to speak to whom; when; where; with what language; tone and volume are the rules and assumptions that constitute the organisation's or team's conversational culture. The taken-for-granted ways we have of talking to each other. There will be reasons for some of the differences: some people just know more about a particular issue; or their seniority gives them a privileged voice. Nothing wrong with that unless these rules are fenced off, part of the forbidden territory of the place. What the senior manager was going to try and what some of the people in this book have tried is to be disobedient and trespass on some of the forbidden spaces. To see if they can get people talking about how they do their talking and if things can be improved to keep people safer.

Structure of the book

To get people to talk about the conversational culture when they already feel silenced and wary is a practical task. There is no lack of guidance about how to speak up and the duty of candour or of reports into the consequences of not doing so. I have not wanted to add to what can be read as a list of 'oughts' and 'shoulds'. The people I know, rate and respect, know they need to speak up. Their question is how the **** do you do that when you are so ****ing anxious you are not sure you even have a voice. I have responded to this challenge by keeping it real, anchored in case examples and keeping modest expectations of what is possible. I have written from a place I know well. A person with no heroic intentions who wants to face that simple and challenging first question—*what is being asked of me right now as I sit with my team in this meeting?*

The case examples are drawn from the English NHS, the wider public and charitable sector, and a smaller number of large commercial organisations. What connects these diverse contexts is the value placed on being part of a team; the pressure to deliver results; work efficiently; keep people safe and often under high levels of intrusive scrutiny and account-ability. The case examples may feel unfamiliar. Hopefully, the behaviours and underlying processes do not; and the suggested interventions worth testing wherever you find yourself.

The case studies are based on exchanges I have witnessed or have been described to me. I have changed details to ensure anonymity. The issues, the tone, the language, and the effects are, I hope, true to what I heard and saw. Some of the case studies are presented in two versions. The first is how things actually played out. The second imagines how a few small changes might have altered the outcome. As you read them, I hope you are able to make links to your own 'cases' and to think about whether anything that is described might be useful.

I have also used my own experiences to explore the origins of our capacity and willingness to speak up and be awkward. I do this to remind myself I am not without sin. I have been the one who has shouted; totally believing I am the only one who sees the way forward. I have been the one who sat in unquiet silence and been on the receiving end of people who definitely knew what was right for me. Again, I hope you make links to your own experience.

Rescuing the bully—the language may offend

I have thought about whether to use the language people have reported. On consideration, I think it's important to remind oneself once in a while of the shock of being told 'to shut the fuck up' in a work setting. Apologies if you are offended.

It can also be a shock to hear someone say this. That the people I see and hear behaving badly can also be people I respect. People doing tough jobs, trying to make complex systems work, under intense and not always kindly scrutiny. Not all. Some are attached to their enforcer image, who enjoy the control. They are in my view, the exception. For the rest, how do we see beyond explanations rooted in character? To find a way to step back from the enforcer role. How do we avoid dismissing them as 'just bullies'? If we do, we also con-sign others to the role of victim and bystander. A situation in which nothing is learnt and nothing changes.

I have assumed we are all a bit safer if I assume we are capable of 'both/and'. I am a victim <u>and</u> a person, in role, with authority and a duty to keep thinking. I am a bullying, rude, fool <u>and</u> capable of a reflexive practice. A bystander sitting in silence like an accomplice <u>and</u> capable of finding my voice: to say, *'we need to stop for a moment and think about how we are behaving'*.

The chapters

Chapter 2: The tyranny of the hospital bed state meeting

There are two versions of this meeting which is at the extreme end of bad behaviour. It involves a capable, usu-ally kind, stressed manager, upon whose shoulders rests the relentless task of managing bed occupancy in a very busy hospital. The first version demonstrates the effects of intemperate behaviour on the 'recipient' and what is lost from the wider task of keeping people safe and delivering contractual compliance.

The second version describes an alternative meeting, anchored in an understanding of what is going on 'below the surface'. Where people find a way to take a step back to think about the complexities of what they are facing as they manage patient flow through a busy hospital.

If you have been that shouty person; or been silenced; or stood by as such an event unfolded, this may give you some clues about why and what can be done. What modest steps to think about, adapt and try—to make it a bit safer to talk about the shared task.

Chapter 3: They would have died anyway

This chapter is based on a very short conversation that resulted in a highly skilled person being silenced for months. It was not the intention but shows that we can be silenced not only by being shouted at and also by a refusal to notice what another person needs.

The second version suggests that a small change of approach can lead to a better outcome for an experienced professional in distress and their busy line manager.

Chapter 4: Not in my name

The focus here is on how a black manager skilfully refuses to do the white executive board's work to understand how discrimination 'works' in their organisation. How someone, who on the surface has less power, exemplifies the role of intermediary. Who is constructively awkward and dislodges the more powerful, so as to create space to think differently.

The second version tries to show what then becomes possible for the board when they recognise that they have failed to take responsibility to think about their thinking; and how this is situated in a raft of unquestioned assumptions.

Chapter 5: The origins of my talk and silence

The previous chapter described the act of a courageous individual, who was constructively awkward. This chapter explores where this capability and willingness to speak and go against grain, may come from. How our upbringing and work experiences may have shaped us. The aim is to develop a capacity to think about how one does one's talking. To understand how one has come to learn about how 'someone like me' should talk. This means thinking about the moments that have shaped this capacity; what I should remember and what I should try and forget, as I anticipate speaking up now in this meeting. To see our talking and ability to resist being silenced as a core skill. How we exercise our agency, leadership and get things done.

Chapter 6: A guide to speaking up

This chapter continues the exploration of what helps to determine our capacity to speak up and resist being silenced. What it may be useful to hold in mind, prior to and during a conversation, as it unfolds. The sort of conversation we think we should be contributing to and when we feel silence may be the safer option. Where even if we opt for silence, we still want to be a good colleague and support other people's efforts to speak.

The roles of follower, bystander and collaborator are described; roles we can occupy without much thought. How to establish psychological safety and the wider responsibility of leadership, both good and bad, is considered. A language is offered to describe types of silence and to describe the effects of bullying and incivility (or 'unprofessional behaviours'). The argument, as in other chapters, is: if we can name things, talking about them is a bit easier.

In section two, attention is on what to think about and try in the moment. The emphasis is on modest interventions anchored in asking good questions. Imposter syndrome is described as a reason 'for not showing up' in a conversation and suggestions are made about how to resist its silencing powers. The difference between 'empathy' and 'compassion' is described, to emphasise the need for practical action. The chapter concludes with a reminder that some work people do is messy and painful and this adds a layer of difficulty when trying to talk.

Chapter 7: Can we talk about our conversational culture?

The last chapter offered ideas to make the best of a situation or context you have found yourself in. Chapter 7 offers ideas and concepts to try and influence the context. To help a team or group think about its conversational culture. To notice, question and modify the explicit and hidden rules and assumptions that shape how to talk to each other around here. Work that means less emphasis needs to be placed on individual capacity to speak up.

The chapter is organised into three sections. The first suggests ways to make the case to managers and senior people, that taking time to review the conversational culture is sensible. Distinction is drawn between types of conversation and their application to the complexity a team may face along with some routine challenges. Questions about how easy it is to learn are raised, and there are reminders about the necessity for psychological safety. Section two imagines you are facilitating a team meeting and what can help make the case to stop and think about the conversational culture. These ideas are presented as slides and through an imaginary facilitator's note-book. Material that can be adapted to create a plan for a team meeting/workshop. Section three assumes the work to engage the team has gone ok and describes ways to keep the conversation going. Given that culture changes slowly, one conversation at a time.

Chapter 8: Walking off the map

This chapter is for senior people who want to try and improve things in their department or organisation. Who understand that trying to contain silencing behaviours through HR procedures, one at a time, is insufficient if you are serious about making it safer for people to talk about what they know.

The chapter is organised into two sections. Section one describes seven mistakes. What to avoid as you contemplate leading an intervention to reduce the use of bullying and incivility to get things done. It is based on a consultancy project I undertook, which did not go to plan because I failed to understand the politics of what I was proposing. The many reasons why a senior leadership can live with other people feeling silenced and unhappy. Section two imagines six steps to an alternative outcome.

This guide can form the basis of the all-important preparatory conversation before action is taken. The planning conversation where ideas are adapted to the context and consequences of success are anticipated.

Chapter 9: Staying hopeful

Being unable to speak is inevitable. This final chapter explores why staying quiet may be the only thing possible at the time, and why that may be. That silence, when an embodied attentiveness, can be a way of offering support during a crisis. An intervention not reliant upon doing a lot of talking. The chapter concludes with a list of things to think about when one is facing silence.

Notes

1 Zeldin, T. (1998) *An intimate history of humanity.* London: Vantage, p. 11.
2 McKie, A. (2004) 'The demolition of man': Lessons from Holocaust literature for the teaching of nursing ethics. *Nursing Ethics*, 11(2), pp. 138–149.
3 There was an interesting article in the Guardian on the 10th December (Bland, 2021) arguing that men and women are judge unequally in terms of the volume of their voice. Men being clear, women being heard as 'strident or difficult'.

    Bland, A. (2021) 'Pushy, gobby, rude': Why do women get penalised for talking loudly at work? *The Guardian*, 10th December [Online]. Available from: www.theguardian.com/lifeandstyle/2021/dec/10/pushy-gobby-rude-why-do-women-get-penalised-for-talking-loudly-at-work (Accessed: 12th December 2021).
4 '. . . *the way for the weak to move the strong is not by force but by modifying their relationship, changing the angle of approach'* (p. 162).

    Zeldin, T. (1998) *An intimate history of humanity.* London: Vantage.

Chapter 2

The tyranny of the
bed state meeting

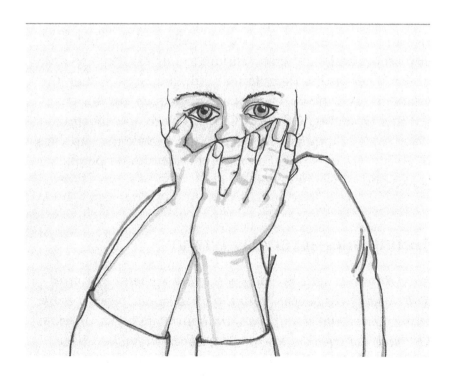

Freedom of speech was an empty right until people freed themselves of the feeling that they did not know how to express themselves properly. . . . They needed first to overcome the old deeply ingrained dislike of being interrupted, which seemed a sort of mutilation. Then they had to be spurred to talk by the need to discuss what they were uncertain about, and by not knowing what to believe [1]

Background

The following story of a meeting to organise the flow of patients through a busy hospital was told to me by Esther, a nurse manager. It may be long forgotten by some of the people who attended it. To me, it's an event that contains many clues and the roles that help explain why bullying and incivility occurs and can be so resistant to our calls to stop and be nice. There is the perpetrator Mark, the target Esther, the bystanders, and the absence of senior people—in this case, the Chief Operating Officer (COO). To study this meeting is to pursue lines of inquiry that force to the surface the variables, not always obvious or easy to see, that determine people's choices and subsequent behaviour.

Meeting one—everyday tyranny

It's the third-bed state meeting of the day, sometime around 15.00. Most of the people around the table have been at work since 7.30 am and doing email an hour or so before at home. Most have not eaten much and have been in back-to-back meetings. The mood is one of tension. Laptops are open and phones being discreetly looked at. The Emergency Department (ED) is backed up and there are not many beds. The divisional manager (DM) Mark, responsible for ED walks in. He sits at the head of the table and notes the senior nurses are sitting together. He calls the meeting to order and starts telling people what he needs to happen.

Mark goes through a list of patients who have been waiting in ED. They need to move to wherever there is an empty bed. One of the senior nurses, Esther, raises a hand. She says she knows Mrs Adams (aged 64) a regular patient on the haematology ward. She is very unwell and needs to go there and not be an outlier. The room quietens. Mark looks at Esther and says that is not possible. Esther persists, 'we cannot ignore the risks . . .'. Mark drops his head and then looks up. 'Look, just ****ing move her. Just do it'. Esther looks away and says nothing more. No one else speaks and the meeting comes to an end with a reminder the next meeting is at 18.00. People understand they will not be leaving work until the crisis is past. Mark leaves. A couple of the other senior nurses stay and ask if Esther is ok. She is visibly upset and feels so for the rest of her day and evening at home.

Consider the same meeting but with a different set of assumptions in the room to explore the idea that what feels inevitable in the scene above does not exhaust what is possible. Small changes are possible and can make things safer to talk about intractable issues, often a site of bad behaviour.

Another version—sharing the anxiety

It's still 15.00 and Mark is still harassed, and people are still anxious and distracted. He feels the pressure to move people to avoid a breach in the ED. He's the one to save the situation and fleetingly wonders why it's always him who has to be the tough guy. People sit around in silence. He hates silence. It looks like you don't know what you are doing. He looks around the room and catches Esther's eye. Hesitant and perhaps angry. He looks at her and gives a slight nod. I must be mad he thinks.

Esther speaks. 'Look, I get the pressure and I know Mark's under huge pressure but (looking at the others) I know there is a risk here we need to face. Outside of this meeting, we will talk about it all but maybe we just need to say it here'. Mark checks his immediate response to tell her to be quiet and reminds himself that she is taking a risk. She is speaking frankly because the situation in the ED requires it. He notes the others' silence for the first time. I wonder if they are going to let her hang.

He wonders at his capacity to be both pissed off and admiring of her. She is really good at holding conflicted situations like this and keeping her cool. He knows he is desperate to get a solution—he has a meeting with the chief operating officer next, who has to respond to the regional director. Who, everyone knows, is a right shouty bastard. Mark realises he is also fed up with the passivity of the people in the meeting. He notes people are looking at him waiting to see what he will do, what he will say.

Esther makes her point about the risk to Mrs A. It makes sense, he can see that, but the pressure remains, and he has his next meeting still in mind. Exhausted with his enforcer image, he asks several people by name for their ideas about managing this dilemma between keeping patients and a patient safer. He is not a clinician.

One of Esther's senior sisters (Chris) offers an idea. 'If Mrs A cannot come to us maybe we can go to her. Why don't I brief the receiving ward on what will help her, while we wait for a bed in haematology?' There are a few nods. Trish another senior nurse looks uncomfortable. Esther asks her to speak. "I'm not sure I'm happy having Chris telling my people what to do." Esther looks cross and is about to express this.

Mark recognises the territorial dispute about to erupt and intervenes. 'We are in crisis, we have a workable solution. You (looking at Esther and Trish) need to work out the details of when and how and what you may need. Brief the group at the morning meeting. We're done, thanks, everybody. See you at 18:00'.

What's different for Mark?

In the first version, Mark's behaviour meets the criteria for bullying. It's the sort of behaviour that reacts poorly to being told 'just be nice'. It's a behaviour that is a persistent part of organisational life. Maybe not in such a gross form but felt in the daily incivilities and aggressions people endure. This is despite our efforts to change things and knowing the impact of such behaviours on wellbeing, thinking and collaboration. And despite our knowledge of the massive financial cost (estimated at £2.281 billion per year in the NHS).[2]

In the second version, he is under the same pressure but has a different approach to managing it. Some of the pressure in the first version comes from the silence. A silence he has enforced by his explosive behaviour. It's an acquiescent defensive silence.[3] The silence we adopt when we think there is nothing we can do here. When intervening and supporting someone like Esther, who we may agree with, is too frightening. To uncertain.

In this second version, Mark is thinking and making connections. The pressure he is under, the role of enforcer which he hates and likes, his frustration with the silence. In this meeting, he accepts that he can only change his behaviour. This is not to deny how fed up he is. While he remains prone to swearing, this is understood as something more than a personal preference or weakness. Culturally it's recognised as a signal that the pressure is getting unbearable. It's not encouraged but it's taken as a communication that should engage people. As in asking—*what can I/we do, what do you need right now, what will help us manage this more safely?*

Rather than being the solution, he is using his authority to lead a process by which people, paid to think about these risks, can speak and thus share the load and responsibility. It's this sharing that reduces the heat of his temper and the risk of shouting and swearing. Of course, to behave differently he has to be less attached to his fixer and enforcer image (and so does everyone else). Something easier to do in a culture that values the capacity of its people to facilitate conversations rather than telling people what to do. Whilst at the same time inviting enquiry when it's unclear what is going on and what is the best thing to do. This is what Schein calls Humble Inquiry:

> 'The skill and the art of drawing someone out, of asking questions to which you do not already know the answer, of building a relationship based on curiosity and interest in the other person'[4]

Mark knows the challenges and he does not know all the answers. He remembers he is not the clinician in the room and that he needs their expertise. He needs to attend to relationships by freeing himself from the assumption that he is a:

> managerial stud, the business athlete who is expected to perform with the minimum of foreplay and only the token acknowledgement of the need for a meaningful relationship.[5]

He could look weak but the invitation to speak is anchored in humility (*I need your know-how*) and authority (*in this public space I am asking you to step forward and take up the authority of your role and advise us*).

What's different for Esther?

In both versions, Esther speaks to what she believes is required of her in the role. Esther is demonstrating a neglected form of leadership. The stubborn refusal to be quiet; to be 'constructively awkward' and speak freely in the face of the threats implied by Mark's language. It's as if, in this situation, she can do no other. She is not the most senior person in the room and has something to lose if she is ignored or 'killed off' by a hostile response.[6] In the first version, she is damaged. She is upset (and remains so for many months) and is left doubting herself.

In the second version, her intervention requires less effort. She is less anxious so more of her cognitive power is available to think about the work in hand, rather than trying to make sense of the abuse. In the first version, she has to overcome her hesitancy to speak; to move from an internal conversation (what is being asked of me here? Oh no. I need to speak) to saying something out loud. In the second version, she takes up the role of intermediary. The way she talks, her obvious concern and knowledge, her understanding of Mark's difficulties, shift his relationship to his authority.[7] She is doing cultural work as well as trying to keep Mrs A safer. She is showing that interruption is not a threat and that 'doing' an inquiry conversation needs practice and tolerance.

Through Esther's intervention, Mark is able to become less concerned with winning and demanding acquiescence and more interested in listening. The way Esther talks makes up for her lack of power. She successfully shifts the focus from Mark to the others and the way they use the informal systems to complain and develop workarounds. Mark knows he is being told that he and the wider group are in danger of missing something and that they should pause and take a breath.

What's different for everyone else?

Mark's first thought is not to question Esther's right to address him, the group, and the issue. Her claim to be heard has been won, at least in this meeting. A claim built on her willingness to see both sides, to face the complexity. The conversation becomes less scripted; being interrupted feels less personal. A diversity of views can be expressed, opening up the possibility of arguing about ideas, rather than people's right to speak.[8] As such the conversation is anchored in the collaborative inquiry described by Schein.[9] Working together they will be more intelligent, raising questions about by-standing and silence.

A significant effect of Esther's intervention, coupled to Mark's lack of overt hostility, is to disrupt how the group uses silence.

As noted previously, silence is an intervention. A means to avoid conflict, a means to flag fear and to protect others. To invite people to speak is to invite them to do their job. In the second version, the senior sister Chris steps forward and offers an idea. She stops by-standing and takes up her authority. As such the group is faced with new information about what is possible. Information that up to this point was hidden in and to the group. Hiding data[10] is a risk activated by bullying and incivility. That is expressed in version one of this meeting and in our organisations daily. What Esther, Mark and Chris are demonstrating in version two is a leadership anchored in talking and helping others to do so. It's not anchored in always knowing.

Summary

The power of the bully is to make people believe there is only one way, their way, of thinking and behaving. Implicitly they argue that the current pressures or 'moment' justify their behaviour. This is the way of the tyrant—to claim a state of exception that warrants the silencing of all criticism. To survive, in the face of bullying, we need to kill off the questioning voice we hear within ourselves.

This silencing is risky in the face of complexity. However, the behaviour of some in the wider system like regulators can contribute to the sense of threat that justifies the state of exception.[11] Which in turn is invoked to justify behaviours that in another context, we have agreed are unacceptable. How else can we explain all the work invested in codes of conduct and improving the work culture?

Significant failures in care have been caused by people being unable to say what they have noticed. Robert Francis, whose report has dominated the NHS safety landscape, noted that *'the word "hindsight" occurs at least 123 times in the transcript of the oral hearings . . . and "benefit of hindsight" 378 times'.*[12] From this, we can assume that we notice more than we routinely talk about and that a focused inquiry will probably reveal more.

Both versions of the story bring into view the role of people not present, the COO, the regulators, patients, and their families. The stories also highlight the role of the bystander. While everyone's behaviour is connected, liberating the bystander is key. Moving from silence to active engagement is a way to mitigate the causes of bullying and reduce its impact when it occurs.

Finally, the stories illustrate the potential of the intermediary. A person who can speak about what may be really going on. Who can name the things that feel hard to talk about and acknowledge this difficulty. Who demonstrate the steadying influence of the intermediary. A capability anchored in useful ideas and concepts. Ideas about what may be going on below the surface. Ideas about what is going on inside people's heads; between people; and the relationship between people and the wider system and task.

Notes

1   Zeldin, T. (1998) *An intimate history of humanity.* London: Vantage, p. 33.

2 Kline, R. and Lewis, D. (2019) The price of fear: Estimating the financial cost of bullying and harassment to the NHS in England. *Public Money & Management*, 39(3), pp. 166–174.

3 Van Dyne et al. (2003) differentiate three types of silence to argue that silence is not the opposite of speaking but is 'strategic and proactive—conscious, purposeful and intentional' (p. 1365). She describes an Acquiescent Silence that withholds relevant information and is associated with disengaged behaviour and sense that one cannot make a difference; a Defensive Silence that omits information because of fear of the consequences of speaking; and a Pro-Social Silence, that omits speaking to protect others.

    Van Dyne, L., Ang, S. and Botero, C. (2003) Conceptualizing employee silence and employee voice as multidimensional constructs. *Journal of Management Studies*, 40(6), September, pp. 1359–1392.

4 Schein, E. (2013) *Humble inquiry. The gentle art of asking instead of telling.* Oakland: Berrett-Koehler Publishers, p. 21.

5 Dartington, T. (2010) *Managing vulnerability.* London: Karnac, p. 374.

6 *Discourse and Truth: the Problematization of Parrhesia: 6 lectures given by Michel Foucault at the University of California at Berkeley, Oct-Nov. 1983.* Available from: https://foucault.info/parrhesia/ (Accessed: 14th December 2020).

7 This is what Zeldin describes as *'the way of the weak to move the strong not by force but by modifying their relationship, changing the angle of approach'* (Zeldin, 1998, p. 162).

    Zeldin, T. (1998) *An intimate history of humanity.* London: Vantage.

8 Edmonson, A. (2012) *Teaming. How organisations learn, innovate bd compete in the knowledge economy.* San Francisco: John Wiley.

9 Schein, E. (2013) *Humble inquiry. The gentle art of asking instead of telling.* Oakland: Berrett-Koehler Publishers.

10 This is what David Hand describes as 'darkened data' (p. 298) when the act of omission is deliberate, which in its extreme form is fraud. It's also about data that we could know if we knew it was missing. Silence, induced by bullying and incivility does not help to keep open questions like 'what else' and 'what's missing?'

Hand, D. (2020) *Dark data. Why what you don't know matters*. Oxford: Princeton University Press.

11 A state of exception names the moment when legislative authority is superseded by executive power. This suspension is based on the claim of a risk and the desire to guarantee the wellbeing of the 'state'. That is a real or imagined way the current order is under threat of collapse, and that chaos is around the corner. This risk is defined by the claimant. They are claiming the power to name the moment of exception and to lead the work to save the current order. A moment that authorises them to suspend the usual rules of discourse and behaviour around here ('breaking the order to save it'—referencing Machiavelli (Agamben, 2005, p. 46)).

Agamben, G. (2005) *State of exception*. London: University of Chicago Press.

12 Francis, R. (2013) *Report of the mid Staffordshire NHS Foundation trust public inquiry*. London: The Stationary Office (HC947). Available from: www.gov.uk/government/uploads/system/uploads/attachment_data/file/279124/0947.pdf (Accessed: 6th January 2021), p. 24.

Chapter 3

They would have died anyway

Death, dying, distress and disease are inescapable
components of a doctor's work. It's hard to see how
it could be otherwise. Excruciatingly difficult tasks
cannot be surgically removed from the daily 'to do'
list of health care staff. What can shift, however, is
our understanding of the psychological demands that
carrying out this work entails.[1]

Bullying and incivility silence in ways we can hear, see and feel. We can also be silenced by a subtle form of quiet coercion, that manifests as a refusal to stop, wait and listen. A refusal that lets us know we are wrong to speak about this, in these terms, with these feelings. The following 'case' explores how this silencing works and what can be done to resist it.

A request refused

It has been a demanding day for the surgical team. The morning started with a long list and the afternoon was shaping up to be challenging. During the afternoon there was a distressing emergency. A young man with a deep laceration. The team worked hard to control the bleeding. Despite their efforts the patient died. Not through any lack of skill but because of the damage they sustained. The place is a mess as the team leave and go their separate ways.

Fast forward two years. I receive a call from Jane,[2] a surgeon on the team. We had met at a workshop where the topic was about how people can be silenced when things do not go well. She said she had not felt able to talk during the workshop, but could we talk now? I agree and we have two conversations, about three weeks apart, lasting in all, two and a half hours.

The first meeting is inconclusive. I feel there is more and that this is a horrific experience. Blood, a lot of blood. However, we have survived the telling. I sat and listened, asked reasonably intelligent questions, she responded coherently; and could bear to listen to herself telling this painful story. I am reminded it's easy to forget, in a professional environment, how hard it can be to talk about feeling overwhelmed; and if one does, the threat this can pose to one's sense of being a good enough practitioner.

The second meeting began with Jane saying she had not talked about what was so awful about this incident. *'I am an experienced doctor. I am used to blood and people dying despite our best efforts. No, things went wrong afterwards'.*

The story unfolded. Jane had bumped into her senior colleague, Carole[3] in the corridor. Jane started to describe what had just gone on. Carole's response was to the point: *'she would have died anyway'.*

Does it have to be like this?

Who knows if Carole intended to shut Jane up, but this is what silently occurred between the two of them. The message was received—*'let's not talk about this'.* You may think all this is not unusual. Carole was just being honest and direct and maybe Jane should just toughen up.

I want to use this chapter to explore how the use of coercive power to silence creates harm. Before doing this, let's dispose of the 'toughen up' argument.

Jane was unable to work and even, for a while, get out of bed. She had children and a husband. They had to look on as she struggled. Her return to work was slow and her sense of herself as a competent clinician damaged, at least for a while. Telling her to toughen up is meaningless advice, anchored in a self-serving stupidity. A refusal to face facts about the nature of work and its effects upon our sense of who we are.

Caroline Elton, quoted at the beginning of this chapter, makes the argument that being a clinician is psychologically demanding. It's worth a moment to appreciate how blindingly obvious this statement is and that it needs repeating. In the many conversations I have had with doctors and nurses I have been struck by the lack of talk about the clinical demands of the job—the laying on of hands and the mess.

Jane and Carole need to be tough to do the work. Their work takes them towards situations that are distressing and difficult. Situations that can *'break through the protective shield of the psyche and cannot be processed'*. To become like *a 'foreign body within the self'*.[4]

'Toughen up' as a means to manage these sorts of situations is simplistic. It's advice rooted in two false assumptions. Professional people don't buckle and break; secondly, if they do, it's about them. That said, these assumptions are sticky. The lack of moral fibre argument has run since Weir Mitchell, a physician in the American Civil War (1861–5), had the heretical thought that fighting a war might have psychological consequences[5] that cannot be dismissed by statements about character.

If I can't say this, what can I say?

If I take the title, status, and salary of manager/leader, I have to find ways of helping people (including myself) manage the psychological consequences of the work. That is, create the conditions for people to do their work well, in sustainable ways. Skilled people like Jane are a valuable resource, expensive to replace and take a lot of time and money to train. There is so much attention on efficiency and saving money, it would be stupid not to do this.

Taking care of people is right but not the only reason why I, as a manager/leader, need to pay attention to these moments of crisis. Jane's intense reaction to events, that seem so rooted in her psyche, is also a clue about how things work around here. So, Carole needs to support Jane but not assume that this is a sufficient discharge of her responsibilities. She needs to interpret this personal moment as a system moment. This requires her to face facts about 'gaps'.

Facts and gaps

As Jane is standing in the corridor, she is in two minds. To talk about her awful experience or to protect herself and Carole from this. Carole resolves this shared dilemma by her intervention. Any further disclosure is discouraged. This silencing has consequences for them both. It also has consequences for the accuracy of their shared understanding about how things work in practice.

This understanding is contingent upon a willingness and capability to do two things. First, to relentlessly think about the four dimensions of work described below.[6] Second, to require and support a conversational culture that authorises questioning and argument, regardless of rank, in the pursuit of intelligent ideas about what is going on.[7] If Carole were to do her job, she would put a real or metaphorical arm around Jane and take her to a safer place. Simultaneously, thinking about what it means for the system she is responsible for creating and leading, that a competent and fearless person like Jane, is suffering so.

Carole struggled with the exchange because she did not have access to a framework that could help her notice and name the sources of data embedded in Jane's personal experience.

Four dimensions of work to keep in mind[8]

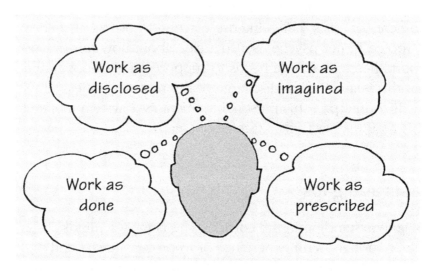

Work as done—is what we do and how we experience our work. Its personal, emergent from our role, training, and experience, and also shaped by policies, objectives, and procedures, usually set by others. There is always a gap between what we do and what is prescribed—the gap between 'policy as written and policy as performed'.[9]

Work as disclosed—is what we say, when asked about our lived experience of our work. We will make a private assessment of what it's safe to say to whom about what. As such, we know more about doing the job than we say. This was the point made by Robert Francis trying to understand why people could appear to tolerate unsafe behaviour in Mid Staffs. He noted that the word 'hindsight' was used 123 times and 'benefit of hindsight' 378 times in written statements.[10]

Work as imagined—if we know more than we disclose there is a gap in the data. We fill this in with our 'reading' of what we hear and our training and experience.

Work as prescribed—based on what we understand to be going on, when in a management/leadership role. We develop policies and procedures and construct a regulatory framework to enforce them, to enable, guide and determine the way work should be done.

Both the opportunity for misunderstanding, as well as the opportunity for a deeper understanding of what it takes to do a job, is embedded in these four 'dimensions'. As such, how people talk to each other and the sense of safety to do so should be the preoccupation of us all.

Relating our story to these four dimensions

One of the things that are going on, while Jane is standing in the corridor in a daze, is what to disclose about her lived experience of doing her job today. This process is private and so makes Carole's job of being supportive and thinking about the wider implications hard.

Jane is having a conversation in her head. It's a conversation with herself, about herself, about what has gone on.[11] Jane is working out how her role and identity as a doctor and surgeon; her sense of being a competent and caring doctor; and her behaviour today 'fits' with this outcome—the death of a young man.

A risk of these entirely normal private deliberations is that they take on the status of the truth about what has gone on. Jane can claim she knows best about what she knows[12] and she can draw erroneous conclusions—*'I'm not a good doctor; I failed; I'm no good'*. Indeed, I think our later conversations were an invitation to challenge this self-orientated explanation. On the day, Carol's short intervention does not dislodge this developing assumption or the emergence of shame. Jane's sense of shame acts like glue—it seals her into her belief it's her fault.

> *Shame can be defined simply as the feeling we have done wrong. It encompasses the whole of ourselves; it generates a wish to hide, to disappear, or even to die.*[13]

This makes it hard for her to speak (disclose) and why Carole's job is so difficult. Jane (and Carole) are both left stranded with her highly edited version of events. I do not know what impression Carole left with, except perhaps that something and nothing had gone on. As they part company, an unacknowledged gap has opened between Jane's experience of doing her job and what has been said out loud.

As Carole walks to her next meeting, half thinking about that and Jane, she faces a question—how to fill in the gaps between what Jane has disclosed and a deeper comprehension of what has gone on? If Carole allows this question to surface in her mind, one way is to guess. To use her imagination to fill in the gaps. This may be an insightful, intuitive leap, based on lots of experience.[14] It may also be based on half recognised prejudice and faulty logic.

If Carole were like Martin in Chapter 2 and you couple a faulty reading with positional, charismatic, or professional power, you have a problem. Carole has the positional power to translate what she thinks is going on into policy and practice. She can tell people what to do, in other words, she can prescribe. Martin bullies people to accept his view of what is going on and his prescription—JFD. Carole can achieve this by the quiet process of silencing.

It's not easy to do Carole's job

Carole faced an ethical moment when she was stopped in the corridor. Does she limit Jane's disclosure or create the conditions for Jane to say more at some point? To subject Jane's thinking to a kind but critical inquiry, to avoid her falling into the personalisation trap (*It's all my fault. If only I was a better. Yes, Jane you're right, it's all your fault*).

We are encouraged to think it's easy to do the right thing. This is unhelpful. We know the times when we should have spoken or intervened and chosen not to do so. With that caveat in mind, to avoid simplistic calls to be nice, what else is possible in this sort of corridor, not much time, situation?

Another version—I'm here

The afternoon still requires the team to do their best they can and to fail. Jane still feels bad and is still in the corridor looking dazed.

Carole sees Jane and stops to ask her what has happened. She sees Jane's hesitation. *'Look I can see you're upset, what happened? I have a few minutes. Let's find somewhere quiet to sit. I want to hear about what went on. I think you were in the new theatre suite this afternoon—how did that go?'*

Who knows if Jane can take up this invitation to talk. Carole would likely have limited time. However, Carole's purpose is not a full debrief but to let Jane know that she knows something has happened to a valued colleague; she is here and will be here to listen over the next few weeks, so there is no hurry.

Carole knows there are no magic words to take away the pain of the events of the day. However, she has to try and prevent Jane from falling down the self-blame rabbit hole. She knows that blaming one person (or allowing them to blame themselves) is always an inadequate explanation and that people like Jane, who are used to and seek out professional autonomy, are prone to blaming themselves.

Carole keeps in mind what Elton said at the beginning of the chapter. The work can be very difficult and have psychological consequences that will need managing, however brilliant a clinician you are. Carole is a surgeon, so knows this to be true. She is like Jane. This helps her identify with Jane, and guess what she might be feeling, but she is wary not to overplay this. As Carole looks at Jane, she knows she is a small step away from feeling her own failures and wanting to push all that away by shutting Jane down. Carole understands she has a choice. She has the authority to exercise discretion and be late for her meeting. To stay, listen and wait. She can also walk away and avoid something awkward and emotional.

Carole stays. She knows that if she does not, much of the cost will be paid by Jane. Carole knows she will lose an opportunity to lead and discover more about working in a context of change that she herself has sanctioned. The opening of the new theatre suite, the decision to move and the way changes are communicated to busy people.

Finally, she knows this is how culture is set. Not through posters on walls but when it hits the fan. When personal vulnerability breaks through professional identity.

The hard task of leadership

In the first version, Carole is attempting to rescue Jane from her distress. This is how she thinks of her management role. Understandable. It's hard not to rescue, but we should not kid ourselves that this is the same as trying to understand what has caused the situation, we think the person needs rescuing from.

Why the caution? Jane does not need rescuing. She needs someone to wait, listen and the opportunity to think and talk with others. Her situation is not just down to her. Her failure to respond positively to being rescued risks her looking bad. Like she is ungrateful or just being difficult. Such a perception will further isolate her, with her distorted reasoning, and make it unlikely there will be any learning about how work happens around here.[15]

Not rescuing but waiting and listening

In the first version, Jane takes up the role that is on offer. It's one of personal failure, morphing into 'hard to help' as she continues to suffer. In the second version, Carole is still confronted by a person in extremis. Still challenged by her desire to tidy things away, under the guise of being helpful. This time she realises that rescuing Jane risks reinforcing her sense of helplessness, triggered by whatever happened.

Carole knows that what is required of her is to get a sense of what has gone on and to work with Jane and others present (and absent) to make sense of it. This is a challenge when your actions as a manager are in the frame. That is why it can be easier to rescue, than stop and face facts. To foreclose the conversation with *'go home and forget it'*. Nothing to worry about here. Superficially, it has the ring of truth, but it hides a deep reluctance to listen.

In this second version, Carole knows that Jane is an adult. A skilled practitioner, having a very bad day. Standing in the corridor in distress does not make her any less capable as a doctor or an adult. Jane, like Carole, is an adult with responsibilities, who wants and needs to find a way back to thinking, to do her job.

This is tough but kind. Kind in the sense of working hard to help someone do their job, to the best of their ability, and holding them to this task. I think this is what Jane missed so much. Her sense of being a competent, capable adult. This event was very hard to bear but it did not have to define her.

What can be useful when faced with distress?

First, give up the idea of a perfect intervention. Good enough is ok. You cannot know in advance how things will play out when people are distressed. That said, here are a few things I have found useful when desperate to help or like Jane, I needed help.

1. Stop, wait, listen

The simple act of being physically present and attentive communicates a recognition of the other person. That they are entitled to this attention; that something has happened; they have feelings, and you can bear to be around them. We all carry the anxiety we will be too much for other people.

You don't even need to say anything massively insightful. Being present is what counts as a form of 'holding'. To just be there when someone is in distress and scared that they may be falling apart. Hearing someone say, 'I'm here'; 'talk to me, it's ok'; 'what do you need?' can be enough.

2. Adapt to the other without assuming they are incapable

Like Carole, you may not have much time, but make time even if it's just five minutes. This communicates your intention to be present. Being clear about how much time offers the other person the opportunity to pace what they say, at what depth and to gather themselves as the time ends. It's easy to under-estimate the thinking power of someone in distress.

3. You're not a therapist but . . .

The moments when things go wrong have the potential to vividly recreate, in the present, a painful event from our past. It's not your job to make these connections, by talking about their past. The task is to help a person reunite with their capacity to think. To work together to link what feels so personal in the way work happens, and is structured and regulated, around here. In this way, you validate people's experience and invite them to be (back) in their role.

4. Be prepared

It should have been no surprise to Carole that one of her people, felt overwhelmed one day. The work is hard and demanding and impacts on people's well-being. No one should waste time arguing this reality, but consider asking yourself:

a. What do people, doing this sort of work, need from their managers, colleagues, and environment to function?
b. What daily behaviours do I need to reliably replicate, to create a sense of psychological safety?[16]

5. Try not to react

Imagine Jane saying—*'whose ****ing stupid idea was it to move theatres?'*—and it was yours. I would be tempted to silence this line of inquiry. This would be a mistake. If I did, I would be setting limits on what can be spoken about, as I encouraged you to open up. Secondly, I would be holding myself to account in the same way Jane is. An adequate explanation of what has gone on is to be found by reviewing lots of actions by people both present and absent.

The problem is if you are successful in waiting and listening, in creating psychological safety, you have to be prepared for people to say stuff that evokes feelings in yourself that may be very uncomfortable for you to hear.

Summary

The work of a manager is hard. You have to hold the tension between getting people to deliver on objectives, and, to comply with policy and practice. You also have to adapt and respond when the environment you have helped develop fails and people feel overwhelmed. The temptation is to walk away under a smokescreen of concern. Jane like Esther in Chapter 2 heard the real message—shut the **** up.

The work of a manager is not to be surprised that environments fail when the task is so challenging. What is important is to stop, wait and listen. To assume that the person who looks so distressed is also capable of being in role and contributing to a conversation about what has really gone on here.

Notes

1 Elton, C. (2018) *Also human. The inner lives of doctors.* London: Heineman, p. 55.
2 Not her real name.
3 Not her real name.
4 Van Der Volk, B. (2014) *The body keeps score. Mind, brain and body in the transformation of trauma.* London: Penguin, p. 327.
5 Holden, W. (1998) *Shell shock. The psychological impact of war.* London: Channel 4 Books.
6 Hollnagel, E., Leonhardt, J., Licu, T. and Shorrock, S. (2013) *From safety-i to safety-II: A white paper.* Brussels, Belgium: EUROCONTROL. Available from: http://skybrary.aero/bookshelf/books/2437.pdf
7 Krammer, E.-H. (2007) *Organizing doubt. Grounded theory, Army units and dealing with dynamic complexity.* Slovenia: Liber & Copenhagen Business School Press, p. 74.
8 See Hollnagel, E. (2017) Can we ever imagine how work is done? *Hindsight*, 25, Summer [Online]. Available from: www.eurocontrol.int/sites/default/files/publication/files/hindsight25.pdf (Accessed: 30th December 2021).
9 Lipsky, M. (2010) *Street level bureaucracy. Dilemmas of individuals in public services.* New York: Russell Sage Foundation, p. xvii.
10 Francis, R. (2013) *Report of the Mid Staffordshire NHS Foundation Trust Public Inquiry.* London: The Stationary Office (HC947). Available from: www.gov.uk/government/uploads/system/uploads/attachment_data/file/279124/0947.pdf (Accessed: 27th January 2021), p. 24.
11 These are described by Archer (2003) as 'reflexive deliberations'.Archer, M. (2003) *Structure, agency and the internal conversation.* Cambridge: Cambridge University Press.

12 They have what Archer calls 'special epistemic status' (2003, p. 50).
13 Lewis, M. (1992) *Shame. The exposed self.* London: The Free Press, p. 2.
14 Intuition is the capacity for rapid and non-conscious reasoning that leads to insight. Insight is making the move from confusion to understanding.

  See Brock, R. (2015) Intuition and insight: To concepts that illuminate the tacit in science education. *Studies in Science Education*, 151(2), pp. 127–167.
15 *Leadership readily becomes equated with rescuing and judged according to its success at alleviating rather than recognizing staff distress. Staff become perceived by leaders as in need of rescue from anxiety and uncertainty and judged accordingly according to their readiness to accept rescue. (p. 7)*

  Blackwell, D. (1997) Holding, containing, and bearing witness: The problem of helpfulness in encounters with torture survivors. *Journal of Social Work Practice*, 11(2), pp. 81–90.
16 *The belief that the work environment is safe for interpersonal risk taking. The concept refers to the feeling of being able speak up with relevant ideas, questions, or concerns. Psychological safety is present when colleagues trust and respect each other and feel able—even obligated—to be candid* (Edmondson, 2019, p. 8).

  Edmonson, A. (2019) *The fearless organisation. Creating psychological safety in the workplace for learning, innovation, and growth.* Hoboken, NJ: Wiley.

Chapter 4

Not in my name

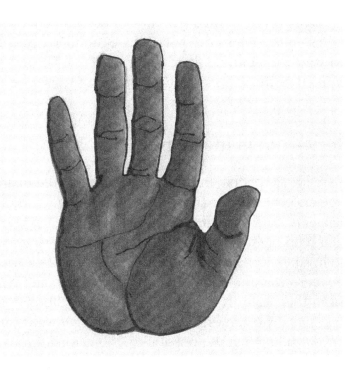

'If I've sinned, I bear the burden of my sins, but only those, and I have more than enough. I don't bear the sins of anybody else'.[1]

DOI: 10.4324/9781003302322-4

Introduction

Bad things happen when we cannot speak. Bad things happen when we cannot bear to listen. Speaking is everything. It is how we link what we think needs to happen to what others think. How we negotiate meaning and what to do next. Therefore, speaking cannot be separated from listening and neither can be separated from the duty of leadership to create and sustain the conditions for both to happen.

The chapter begins with a story of an act of individual resistance in a board meeting. The story of a black manager, refusing to collude with the group's wish to avoid looking at their thinking and behaviour. The story is told as it happened and is reworked to highlight the interaction between speaking and listening. What is required if we are to be 'constructively awkward'; to cultivate the capacity to resist. Second, what is required of those present at a moment of resistance.

Story—not in my name

There are 20 people in the room. Present is the board of this large and complex organisation and a small group of its senior managers. The managers have, over the past few months, been working together to find ways of expressing more of the lived experience of their work. To try and narrow the gap between what the board imagine is going on and what it takes to run this place. The atmosphere is slightly formal, hierarchy is present. The conversation moves slowly towards an explicit conversation about the possibility of breaking through the standard narrative about how great this place is. It is and that is not the only experience in the room today.

The catalyst for the work had been a previous session, led by a community activist and leader. He epitomised what it was to be constructively awkward; to speak up about what and who may be silenced and ignored in the way everyday life unfolded in communities. Communities in which the silent assumption of whiteness blocked conversations about what different communities needed to thrive.[2]

His daily life was about how power played out in communities. He spoke kindly, without fuss. You got the sense of a man who lived his words. Tough, brave, and purposeful.

His stories and his manner of talking, unlocked experiences that had been silent in the group. He enabled people to go where the hidden difficulties were in this group of talented leaders, serving a large and diverse community.

Back into the room

A board member asked Ime what they needed to do to stop marginalising people (like him). What had been an abstract conversation about difference became real. It was now in the room. Ime spoke.

He said he wanted people to stop behaving as if he knew the answer to racism and discrimination. It was not his problem. He was on the receiving end of these behaviours. He understood people wanted to understand why discrimination occurred in the organisation, despite the campaigns to stop it. He knew they knew these behaviours hurt people. However, why did people insist on asking him about what needed to be different; when it was their lack of insight into their own behaviour that contributed to the problem of discrimination he and others felt? He wondered if people could stop working on this issue through him. He was exhausted with it. Every day required a massive effort to fit in and not retaliate. He stopped and waited.

This was a moment

Earlier chapters focused on people being silenced, through being ignored or shouted at. Ime refused to be silent.

Somehow, at this moment he confronted a group of power-ful people. Good people prone to wilful and unconscious ignorance about their impact on others, about what can be said. Ime exemplified the sort of resistance that encourages people to stop and enables them to think.[3] No shouting, no swearing, no quiet avoidance. Just a clear 'stop', 'wait', 'let's think about this'.

An uncomfortable truth

Ime exemplifies the level of effort required of people, sub-ject to the oppressive use of power. The effort required to speak your mind. To name what you think is going on; who is being ignored; to what effect. He spoke an uncomfortable truth 'cleanly' and there was a sense of discomfort; of being caught out in an assumption about who and what was the problem.

Ime called attention to the assumption that hearing about his experience of discrimination would be enough to under-stand the motivation to discriminate. He was pointing to the possibility that the intention to talk about discrimination was a means to keep things the same. A means to keep the assumptive scaffolding quietly embedded in the fabric of the organisation.

There followed a conversation about how people were thinking and feeling. It lacked substance as if its purpose were to fill time, as people privately thought about what had been said. It became clear it would not be possible to take up the challenge. To think about how one person was being asked to do the work for the majority and had said 'no'.

That said, in the closing plenary some people realised they had been asked to grow up. To face the fact of their depen-dency on someone else, Ime, to make things better. To face the fact this dependency drained them of their power to inquire into their part in what was going on.

Same moment heard differently

We are in the same room, same people and Ime has said what he said. This time the board members (remember there were also a few senior colleagues of Ime present) invoke the principle of stop, wait and listen.

The shock of the comment is acknowledged by the board chair (Sir Tim). Not in that neat dismissive way of, *'thank you so much for that insightful comment . . . what's next on the agenda?'* No, more of a statement about how he is feeling. A couple of sentences, based on his internal conversation (*Oh **** this is a moment, shit, my mind is blank, I need to say something, hurry up . . .*), spoken out loud to set the tone of the conversation required to face this moment.

Sir Tim speaks:

I feel like I have been told something I am finding hard to hear, made worse by thinking I should know it already. I know this is not your intention Ime, but I find myself short of words. I know it took a lot to say that. Respect but we (moving his gaze from Ime to the wider group) need to take it slow. Who can help us think about this?

Let us imagine the director of HR (Jo) has done some thinking and reading. She has waited for this opportunity—it's not as if it has been easy being a woman on the board.

Jo speaks:

Ok, I will have a go. We have been around this issue so many times. We have to stop. We keep putting people in a difficult place. Ime has been at pains to not use 'racism'. I know we do not want to hear this but maybe it's the right word. I can see how uncomfortable some of us are with this word but let's face it what we have been told is not a surprise. If it's not a surprise, what have we done with this knowledge? We have done what we tend to do when we reach moments like this—we ask for more data. I want to suggest we try something else.

Jo stops and looks at Sir Tim.

Sir Tim:

Keep going Jo.

Jo:

We have to think about how we have built into the very fabric of our organisation, via our everyday conversations, subtle ways of communicating, replicating, and reinforcing what 'we' as a white leadership group take to be the right and normal way to think and act around here.

A few people are drifting off at this point, silently thinking it's too managerial; too soft; not relevant to me. I'm not racist; my job is audit. I might just check my phone; no, I will send a WhatsApp to John opposite—see what he is making of all this.

Of course, in the room there is silence, just Jo speaking. Jo is feeling out on a limb. Experiencing some of what it feels

like to go against the grain in this culture.⁴ It's not comfortable. Despite Sir Tim's words of encouragement. Important in
terms of authorising the conversation but Jo is looking to her
fellow directors and the CEO, Charles.

Charles can see the continuing discomfort of Jo. His
silence if it continues will be heard as *'we're not going to do
this now'*. He knows he likes to control conversations but
there are risks if he silences Jo and Ime. People will talk outside of the meeting. He looks around the table at his team.
Over half a million to pay this lot. Why do I have to do all
the thinking? Jo is right we have worked our way around this
issue for too long.

Charles:

*Ime thank you. Jo thank you. Jo, can you say more?
I'm like Tim (smiling), I'm struggling because the
implication is I'm part of the problem but it's hard
to think about your thinking and what's missing. We
have about 30 minutes left. I also want to say this is
a difficult conversation so let's keep it in the room for
the moment and operate under the Chatham House
rule. Anyone disagree? Ok good. Jo?*

Jo:

*This is what you pay me for so I will be direct. This
is what I think. Our current approach is shallow. We
count individual incidents of discrimination. We act
after the event. What we do not do, as I said earlier,
is to investigate how our everyday ways of talking
and thinking create a culture that some people feel
excluded by. A culture, where some people feel they
have to fit, or risk being seen as different and not in a
good way.*

*We keep asking people, subject to our leadership;
our assumptions, about how that feels. That has to
stop. That is what Ime is saying. We need to stop looking to others for clues and face facts. We set the culture and we (looking around the room) look similar,
sound similar and share many common experiences.*

*I know we hate not knowing what to do but we can
take control of how we do this—find a way to learn
about how we, as the leadership group, create the conditions that lead some people to feel unwelcome and
the pressure to fit in. How we marginalise and silence
some conversations. Not sure how, we just need to stop
asking the people who are the victims of this process to
say more about the experience of being marginalised.
It's unethical. We need to work out our approach.*

Charles:

*Jo, thank you. I have a suggestion. We do an Open
Space conversation to explore a question—something
like . . .' If people felt safer, what would they say about
how we can silence and side-line people around here?
It needs work but this is where we need to go, I think.
We need to end the meeting. Thank you Ime and
thank you, Jo. Brave work.*

Moving on from dependency to dependence[5]

The words spoken by Jo (and the understanding of the intention of Ime's intervention) were informed by the writing of
Eddo-Lodge.[6] She draws attention to how people subject to
oppression, are further oppressed by the relentless questioning
of their experience. It happens in matters of race and people
who have been bullied. She argues that answers do not lie
with more questions:

*I still think there is a communication gap, and I'm
not sure if we will overcome it. Even now when I talk
about racism, the response from white people is to
shift the focus away from complicity and on to a conversation about what it means to be black, and about
black identity*

(*p. 214*)

A way of thinking about this gap between what the board
imagine and what Ime discloses about his experience of work
is to differentiate between dependency and dependence.
Dependency is expressed by the board in the first version.
They act as if they share the unspoken assumption that only
Ime can sort this complex issue of 'race' out. This will drain
any sense of agency in the group. Such a shared assumption
is also defensive. It's anchored in the anticipation of and need
to avoid the uncontained eruption into conscious awareness of
the anxiety attached to racism and difference. This is a sophisticated group, working in a sophisticated way to lose their
minds. To not think and wait for rescue like tourists caught
out by a fast-rising tide. Ime wisely sees the danger of heroic
rescue and attempts to shift the group back into thinking or
work mode by testing the capacity for dependence.

The second version imagines this shift has been modestly
successful. Sir Tim's intervention is in the mode of stop, wait
and listen. He acknowledges how he is feeling; perhaps suggesting to others that feeling uncertain, struggling to hear is
data. Data about what they are not thinking about. Such a
thought takes back the assumption that Ime has the answer.
That may be the group also has intelligence and can think
about what might be going on. That such a complex issue
needs collective learning and thus will not be easy. The group
will have to go to where the difficulties are. As Jo says gender
difference is also shaping who can talk to whom, about what,
with what words and tone.

As the group goes on to talk about what it already knows it's practising dependence. They need Jo to speak and guide, they need each other to encourage and contain. They are trying to learn as they go as they recognise issues of difference and how they are managed are already part of their process, ways of talking and organising things. They can choose to talk about this or not. If they do, they risk learning things that will require change.

Leadership of ignorance

Leadership is too easily associated with knowing what to do. How to answer the questions, solve difficult problems. This is a dimension of leadership but insufficient. Ed Schein has a way of framing ignorance that makes it easier to hear when you're senior. He argues that skilful leaders know when they do not know the answer. That the issue to be faced is complex. That, whatever you decide, you will act with insufficient data; and however well planned the intervention, there will be unintended consequences that will need managing. Such leaders are capable of humility. An approach that:

> *derives from an attitude of interest and curiosity. It implies a desire to build a relationship that will lead to more open communication . . . that one makes oneself vulnerable.*[7]

The way I imagine Tim and Charles talking is that they know this is a moment for humility. To use their authority to enable a conversation. To relinquish, at least for the moment, any wish to tell people what to think. That the work is the conversation as a means to swap and develop ideas and to notice how this work happens as a way of tracking silent assumption about who gets to speak to whom etc. This is the leadership of process, and it's tough work for smart people, who like to know and if they don't, frame the issue in ways that fit their preferred ways of thinking and behaving.

Learning at this level, together makes us anxious. Anxious about our status and competence as learned professionals and the validity of our assumptions and knowledge.[8] As such, resistance is an understandable response when our assumptive frameworks are put into doubt. Even if we choose to do this.

Ime was only stating the obvious and doing so in a sophisticated way. This was a white group, leading a diverse workforce. Their whiteness, their shared assumptions, will cause them to struggle to hear some people's lived experience. They can sit in silence, safe in the assumption that the world was pretty much as they like it and know it. That they could fill in the gaps about other people's experience of their organisation with their situated imaginings. Ime's intervention was a reminder of these facts. More painful was his implied observation that the group hid this assumption of 'whiteness' from itself.

Charles, as CEO, suggesting an Open Space[9] conversation is in the bounds of possibilities. It's a well-tested structure, to explore topics characterised by diverse and conflicting perspectives. Where people want to explore how power works around here. It's an approach that contains anxiety by having a clear structure and process. A methodology that enables a willing leadership team to step back and not seek to predetermine outcomes or define what and who is good and acceptable.

A sophisticated leader like Charles uses this sort of approach to signal two things. To signal the senior team's shift to deep learning. To publicly excavate and critically evaluate the assumptions that underpin its approach and test these in terms of their effects upon others' thinking and behaviour. In this case on their ability to deliver safe care across diverse communities. Secondly, that he has a responsibility to hold his executive team to the learning task, by making it safe enough for them to do this hard cognitive, emotional work. Kindly insisting this work is done; asking what they need, and not second-guessing what that works looks and sounds like.

Closing comments

The justified criticism of this sort of imaginary narrative is that it fails to face facts. It's very hard to speak to and confront the dominant ways of thinking and behaving if one is also part of that group. That said, the risk of speaking up is no greater than what Ime faced, and he spoke anyway. His intervention is not made up, nor is the context even if the names have been changed. Ime was not a superman, he had just had enough, felt he was talking for others and saw an opportunity. You can argue that Jo was similarly capable.

Ime spoke to what was missing in the way people could think. He had a hard message but did not shout or swear. His authority came from lived experience and exasperation with current thinking and behaviour. He was tactical. The workshop was about thinking and learning together. This made it less likely people would counter with positional power and sanctions. His approach exemplified what Zeldin calls *'the way of the weak'*.[10] Ime did not meet these very senior people head-on. His tone, his words were sufficiently clear and anchored that (some) people's approach to the subject of race was disturbed. They stopped and saw a different possibility, as I imagine a rock climber might look up a rock face and see different routes to the top.

He got people who were not thinking, who were not aware of their not thinking, to think and in a modest way do this together. His intervention was an act of leadership. A display of quiet refusal of the preferred way that had evolved to judge people. An act of resistance.

Notes

1 Levi, P. (2000) *If not now, when?* London: Penguin, p. 128.
2 Macalpine and Marsh (2005) add a dimension to the meaning of silence and the effects of context on empowerment. They consider the experience of minority groups. Being gay or black can feel wrong in the face of the silent assumption of hetero-sexuality and whiteness. They argue that in these situations, power is expressed through the silence. This is silence as discourse which authorises certain ways of talking and thinking. This boundary is maintained by self-policing as embarrassment or fear. This makes it harder to question how language and practice,

> '. . . *discursively conceals what would be otherwise be so noticeable—the continued huge disjuncture in power/status/life chances between black and white people*'
> *(Macalpine and Marsh, 2005, p. 443)*.

Macalpine, M. and Marsh, S. (2005) On being white: There is nothing I can say. Exploring whiteness and power in organizations. *Management Learning*, 36(4), pp. 429–450.
3 This is 'situational resistance'. Situational resistance is expressed by people resisting the current position, custom and practice. People draw attention to what is missing or inadequate (and survive).

See Caygill, H. (2013) *On resistance. A philosophy of defiance.* London: Bloomsbury.
4 To recognize to go against the grain is hard It risks further exclusion and confronting the daily . . . *silently raised eyebrows, the implicit biases, snap judgment made on perceptions of competency (Edo-Lodge, 2018, p. 64.)*.

Eddo-Lodge, R. (2018) *Why I'm no longer talking to white people about race.* London: Bloomsbury Publishing.
5 See Dartington, T. (2010) *Managing vulnerability.* London: Karnac. See chapter 4.
6 Eddo-Lodge, R. (2018) *Why I'm no longer talking to white people about race.* London: Bloomsbury Publishing.
7 Schein, E. (2018) *Humble leadership. The power of relationships, openness, and trust.* San Francisco: Berrett-Koehler, p. 19.

8 See Argyris, A. (2000) *Flawed advice and the management trap*. Oxford: Oxford University Press.

Argyris, C. (1991) Teaching smart people to learn. *Harvard Business Review*, 69(3), May–June, pp. 99–109.

Argyris, C. (1986) Skilled incompetence. *Harvard Business Review*, 64(5), September–October, pp. 74–79.

9 Owen, H. (1992) *Open Space Technology*. Potomac: Abbott Publishing.

10 Zeldin, T. (1998) *An intimate history of humanity*. London: Vantage, p. 162.

Chapter 5

The origins of my talk and silence

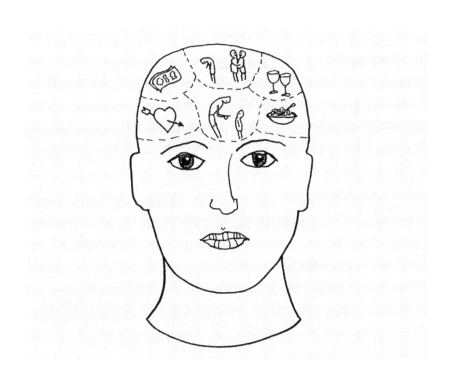

DOI: 10.4324/9781003302322-5

'We have to call time on the bullshit that makes us feel as if we are powerless, the bullshit that tells ordinary people they have a defined place in the world and should put up with their lot'.[1]

Introduction

There are people like Jess Phillips who embody bravery, who take a stand. During the course of my DProf, I interviewed ten people who, like Phillips, had taken a stand. Calling out racism in a school; racism in the police service; poor clinical practice; gaps in thinking; the use of mobile phones on the 8.15 from Oxford. They did not consider themselves heroic. They remembered the times they had not spoken more often than the times when they had spoken. In my view, if not heroic, definitely kind, and tough people, capable of being splendidly stubborn, awkward, and argumentative.

My research was to understand how leaders authorised themselves to be 'constructively awkward'.[2] To question how sense was being made; to draw attention to who or what may be silent; who or what may be at risk and do it in a way that helped people think. As I worked on my research, I wanted to understand how we come to know how we should speak. What helped determine a willingness to speak, to go against the grain and resist silence? More specifically, as a person with an average score in terms of speaking up and choosing to be quiet, what has influenced me?

As I look back at my younger self, as a white, male, European child, what have been the 'moments' that shaped my capacity to speak, question and resist silence? How had family, education and work shaped my willingness to question, be a bit awkward?

This modest exploration of self is important. To know how one has been inducted into the world of talking and listening is to be reminded that conversation is a cultural act. Permeated with hard to see and hear rules about what correct talking is. Rules about how people like me, should talk to someone like you, with what words and tone about what. And what we should do and avoid when disagreement threatens to surface. If I can 'see' these rules I can choose what ones to follow and what ones are there to keep me quiet, from doing my job to the best of my ability.

You will have your own stories, ideas and theories. I hope you will bring these to mind, noticing how you have been inducted. Remember try to be kind to yourself. My experience of this sort of recall is to also dredge up events I did not and do not feel good about, based on what I know now at 64. Such is the task of learning as an adult.

Stories of growing up

School

My earliest memory of the politics of talking and silence was when I was about five. Walking with my mother to go shopping. My mother meeting a neighbour. After the conversation, my mother told me off for sticking my tongue out. That this was rude. Even now I remember the sense that my protest was in vain. Her word was the word.

I was sent to Prep school when I was seven. I enjoyed it and continued my induction into the world of talking and silence. The schoolteachers expected obedience. They set the tone on what could be said to whom about what and when. Being good was being quiet and not asking questions. I learnt to wait for my turn, sit quietly, to learn. Useful skills. I also learnt about the culture of conversation associated with my class, gender and ethnicity. Now I understand how these rules aligned and reinforced my brain's (hardening) wiring to lean towards compliance. To fit in, suppress my difference and notice the hierarchy in the room.[3] I learnt to self-police my internal dissenting voice, such as it was.

The capacity for conformity is useful. I can work as part of the group. I can suppress my desire to always question; talk over people; wait my turn; have it my way. I can help get things done with others. However, there is a downside to this 'fitting in'. An inclination to unthinking compliance and a conscious suppression of doubt.

My bike

I was a keen cyclist. One day I was riding around the local park, when three kids took my bike and refused to give it back. I felt impotent and uncertain. Eventually, they gave it back and I rode home. As I put my bike away, my dad asked me what was wrong. I started crying. He said to get into the car. He drove me to the park and said to hit the biggest one. I did. The others ran off. I got back into the car.

My dad rarely interfered. My brother and I had amazing amounts of freedom as we grew up. The astute reader will realise it was not a simple lesson. It was about standing up for oneself, knowing I was capable of saying no. The aggressive assertion of what I took to be my rights. A lesson about not getting carried away with asserting my rights and a reminder of my deference to authority. While I was surprised and anxious about my father's words, I did not stop to think about the consequences or alternatives. The enduring lesson was moments like these are not simple. You have to work out what the meaning is and what is the right thing to do.

An enduring memory was being present in the moment. I was alone, the outcome was uncertain (would they run away so easily?) and whatever happened there would be consequences and they would need managing (what if I was the one to get hurt?). An induction into the uncertainty of speaking up in adult life.

Death in the family

It has been 43 years since by brother died. Suddenly, quietly at home. The disruption of our comfortable safe life was profound. Time enabled an adjustment to this new reality. It was an adjustment partly achieved by going quiet. Entering a dissociative state, to disconnect from troubling emotions, that were hard to name. A phrase I heard a lot from the grown-ups was—*'it's time to get back to normal'*. Even then I heard this as—*'I don't really know what to say, so I will invoke a hypothetical state called normal and ask you to go quietly and occupy it'*.

Student nurse

The place I really started to think about my capacity for compliance was on my first placement as a student nurse. I was 19. I had worked as a nursing auxiliary on a male surgical ward at my local hospital. The nurses there took a lot of trouble to teach me. To show me stuff and to encourage me to think about nursing.

Now I am a student nurse in a busy acute admission ward in a psychiatric hospital. I want to belong but as a first-year student feel on the outside. I learn not to talk about how awful it is to have no idea what I am doing or supposed to do. That this can be a scary place and sometimes violent place. I learn to suppress my feelings, toughen up and not question some of the methods I see. I model myself on Jeff the junior charge nurse. Male, funny and a reputation for being a bit loud and confrontational. He seems confident to me. He is the one to lead any confrontations.

Much later I am walking down the long corridor of a hospital that is closing. It is 2:00 am and I am here to talk to the night staff about redeployment. I had expected to find them indifferent. I found people who cared as best they could, within the architectures, rules and expectations of the institution. A place where some patients had been confined for most of their adult lives and some subject to invasive treatments. It got me thinking about being a student nurse again and what it was to be part of this profession. A profession that had not always questioned what was taken to be kind and appropriate treatments.

I knew about the reality of asylums and had worked as part of that system of care and control. I may have questioned, but mostly I went along with the prevailing attitudes and behaviours. The consequence of my silence, my passive followership, on occasions a lack of kindness. I can argue the degree, that I was part of a team in an institution but suffering is still suffering.

Years later, I am reading the report by Robert Francis.[4] He comments on how often the phrase 'benefit of hindsight' is used in the evidence. I am reminded of my capacity to be quiet, when I should speak because I have seen or heard something that doesn't feel right. The capacity to quietly weigh speaking up, belonging, feeling stupid and the risk of being evicted from the group. The tension between being the person, the nurse, I want to be and what I do day to day. As I read, I know it is not only about the people in the report. I have to face facts. I can and have blocked my ears and covered my eyes, to not see the discomfort and pain of others. I can be that docile follower. I need to be vigilant.

Stories—of work

It is not only others who shout

I am the director of an organisation providing residential and nursing home care. I am in my office with the Director of Finance (FD) and Director of HR. We are trying to agree on how we can devolve more power to the managers running the services close to the clients. I half grudgingly acknowledged the reasons why the central team is not keen. They argue we are putting compliance at risk. I do not want to think about this. Instead, I dismiss their concerns as vested interest. They like telling the house managers what to do. I am not wrong, but I am not right either.

The FD has unwittingly taken up their cause. As we struggle with what to do, he repeats the phrase—*we can't do that*—several times. The frustration I feel erupts and I hear myself shouting. I can see the shock cross his face and he and the HR director go quiet. I apologise and repeat it the next day, but we do not recover. He rightly feels that he has been the recipient of my frustration that does not entirely belong with him. I should have been able to take a step back. I have to face another fact. Faced with a situation, in which someone who I think I can rely on, keeps saying no, I can hear it as a dismissal. One that feels like being told to go quietly, to go back to normal.

I do not believe I behaved well; and I think such moments are inevitable if you take your work seriously and need others. The past will erupt in the present. As if I were talking to someone from the past, as I shouted at my colleague, re-enacting a time I felt a profound sense of being ignored.

This was an important event that was personal and had systemic meaning. I would have to work harder to notice when I was acting out the past. To accept that silencing and bullying was not something others did. I could do it. I had to learn how to see the substantive systemic issues hidden in the fight. The fracture in our relationship pointed to what we should have been talking about.

How were people to reorientate themselves to this new approach? Change in a way that allowed them to stop doing what they were doing and for that to feel ok. To change and have strong professional identities and have their questions heard. My failure was shutting off this conversation. Making it personal between me and the FD, leaving no space to hold the centre team to account. To ask them to engage their professional know-how so we could face the ethical question of the good of our clients.

I now think this experience was inevitable. I lacked the skills to insist we stop and think in the midst of this difficult, heated conversation. This next event showed me that it is possible to disrupt a line of thinking, contain the inevitable emotional consequences and to think.

A short sharp shock

This is a moment I think about when I need to be braver than I feel. To say something that I think will land unpredictably. That will have consequences, I will need to think about and respond to at the moment. When I may be at risk of being rude or bullying because the stakes are high and time is short.

I have been asked to act up as the CEO. In an organisation where I had been for about a year, in the role of care manager. I was delighted and anxious. I arrived at my session expecting sympathy. To be reassured, my anxiety diminished. This did not happen. What did is captured in the follow-up note to our conversation:

> You haven't had much management experience, or experience of the organisation, and we were seeing your Care Manager role as a challenge to learn to think as a manager as well as a consultant. Suddenly you find yourself in a position of a chief executive. It's not surprising that you feel panicky and sometimes overwhelmed.
>
> I say, 'find yourself', but of course you did have sufficient confidence in yourself to accept the job. You talked as though you really were the chief executive now and can introduce whatever programmes you think fit. What do you make of that?

The key sentence was: *"find yourself", but of course you did have sufficient confidence in yourself to accept the job'.* I was so cross. Not adult cross. 3-year-old how dare you not make me feel better immediately, cross.

While I calmed down, he sat there and waited. The sense of containment eventually permeated my infantile rage. I became an adult again and my capacity to think returned. As we talked the underlying cause of my anxiety surfaced as I realised, I could talk about it, even though I felt stupid.

First of all, I had placed myself in this position. I wanted to be the CEO. I knew it was a big step but I thought I had the skills to do it; and as I anticipated this step, my confidence just evaporated. I could hardly bear to think about my ignorance. However, adopting a hubristic, blustering style, feeling like an imposter didn't appeal either. The substantive issue was authority.

The role was an acting one. At a practical level, I needed to know what I was authorised by the board to do. To have a conversation about what issues I could tackle and how often I needed to talk to them to get reauthorised. I also needed to think about how I authorised myself. How I thought and felt about being a leader, being responsible. What sources of power could I access and how would I keep my doubt in view and not fall into bluster?

This conversation was years ago. It embodies one of those moments I learnt something useful. How to challenge, knowing what is said will initially at least be unwelcomed and that this will be expressed as we tackle this important issue. I had hoped to be comforted. My supervisor spoke assuming I was in role. That this was work time. What I needed was a different perspective. To have my preferred interpretation of what was going on dislodged. To check if other perspectives might give better traction on the substantive issue of me in a leadership role.

My final thought about this conversation is it confronts me with my desire to be nice, empathetic and doing something useful. To be kind and compassionate. I will discuss this tension in Chapter 7.

Stories of home

My noisy neighbours

Up to this evening, I had not consciously understood that speaking up did not have to be a solitary act. Something I have to do because something about me was being questioned. This was a moment about the place others can play in helping us speak.

It is 3:00 am and the students in the house that backs onto our garden in Cambridge are partying hard. I am trying to ignore their loud voices but stay awake until about 4:40 am.

Next morning, I ask my elderly neighbour if she had been kept awake. She had. She seemed pretty fed up. Next night, the same party. This time I get up and go around. I am noticing the adrenaline and keep a check on my language and volume as I ask them to quieten down. They are very drunk. I return the following morning, saying their behaviour is upsetting people. That they need to respect the neighbourhood. They agree; at least for a few days.

I think if I had not had my neighbour in mind, I think I would have either put up with it or got into a shouting match. An avoidance of what was required. A conversation about enjoying yourself with others, noise, neighbours and time of day.

Acting on behalf of others, was significant for the people I interviewed. They said it often drove them to speak. It helped overcome their reticence to intervene. It seems important that this 'other' is real. They have a face, a name. Someone we can positively identify with. Someone who evokes a state of compassion in us. An identification that pushes me out of a passive sense of 'how awful' to action.

This final story is a reminder of how important it is to have another person in mind. It is also a reminder of how normal self-doubt is when deciding if to speak or stay quiet.

A footpath incident

I was walking back to my house one evening. The light was low as I turned down the footpath. I heard then saw a man urinating. I became preoccupied with two thoughts. That he was also on the phone, having a loud conversation and that this was a moment. The day's news was of the murder of Sarah Everard; male behaviour in public places; and the duty of men to call it out.

All this registered in seconds as I walked past him. I said nothing. I rehearse all kinds of things I wanted to say but mostly I am relieved. I will not get into a fight, which has happened before. Mostly I feel useless. I think about this incident for several days and why I failed.

The obvious explanation based on the chapter so far is that this situation lacked another person. In my ruminations I wondered if I would have said something if I was with my 91-year-old mother who lived nearby. Probably.

The strangest thing was I was asking myself, was this really happening. Had I in some way mis-read the situation. Self-doubt was frequently described by the people I interviewed. People capable of challenge in high volatile situations. It was so frequently mentioned I took it to be a normal part of speaking up. A conclusion that weaned me of the heroic model of speaking up.

Conclusion

Speaking up is a cultural act. Something we are taught how to do. As we grow up, if we are lucky, we can see how we have been enabled and constrained in this fundamental skill. We learn to think and act for ourselves. Each time I speak up, to question what is going on I am anchored in the moments described here. That as I open my mouth, these events and others have helped me get to this moment. That is why it is important to do an inventory of your own events and moments.

To stand back and ask:

1. What have I learnt about how someone like me should talk?
2. What helps and what do I need to forget?
3. What else do I need to learn and practice to say more?
4. When I have spoken up, what was going on?

Notes

1   Phillips, J. (2019) *Truth to power. 7 ways to call time on B.S.* London: Hachette, p. 12.
2   Naylor, D. (2008) *An investigation into how public sector and community-based practitioners authorise constructively awkward intentions.* DProf thesis. London: University of Middlesex [Online]. Available from: https://eprints.mdx.ac.uk/6894/ (Accessed: 18th June 2021).
3   See Eagleman, D. (2015) *The brain. The story of you.* Edinburgh: Canongate Books.
4   *Between 2005 and 2008 conditions of appalling care were able to flourish in the main hospital serving the people of Stafford and its surrounding area. During this period, this hospital was managed by a Board which succeeded in leading its Trust1 (the Mid Staffordshire General Hospital NHS Trust) to foundation trust (FT) status. The Board was one which had largely replaced its predecessor because of concerns about the then NHS Trust's performance. In preparation for its application for FT status, the Trust had been scrutinised by the local Strategic Health Authority (SHA) and the Department of Health (DH).*

Monitor (the independent regulator of NHS foundation trusts) had subjected it to assessment. It appeared largely compliant with the then applicable standards regulated by the Healthcare Commission (HCC). It had been rated by the NHS Litigation Authority (NHSLA) for its risk management. Local scrutiny committees and public involvement groups detected no systemic failings. In the end, the truth was uncovered in part by attention being paid to the true implications of its mortality rates, but mainly because of the persistent complaints made by an incredibly determined group of patients and those close to them. This group wanted to know why they and their loved ones had been failed so badly. (p. 7)

Francis, R. (2013) *Report of the mid Staffordshire NHS foundation trust public inquiry.* London: The Stationary Office (HC947). Available from: www.gov.uk/government/uploads/system/uploads/attachment_data/file/279124/0947.pdf (Accessed: 20th March 2021).

Chapter 6

A guide to speaking up

DOI: 10.4324/9781003302322-6

On a map the weather is always good, the visibility perfect. A map offers you the power of perspective over a landscape: reading one is like flying over a country in an aeroplane—a deodorized, pressurised, temperature-controlled survey. But a map can never replicate the ground itself.[1]

Introduction

This chapter offers a guide for navigating those meetings and conversations in which you want to find and keep your voice. Where you suspect that what you have to say will be contested. Where you may slip into an acquiescent silence because of real and imagined worries about not staying quiet. It is a guide for people who want to play their part. Who want to support others taking the risk to question what is assumed to be normal and right around here. Who want to let them know they are not alone, that they are in an organisation that will not leave them hanging. The sort of colleague who knows speaking up, resisting silence is a team effort.

The chapter is organised into two sections. The first is a set of ideas and skills to think about if you know that, at some point, someone is going to have to say something. When silence will mean, the same old stuff will just keep happening; and people will be in the corridor, saying how awful things are and something has to change.

The second section is a set of ideas to hold in mind as you work in the moment of a difficult meeting or conversation. When you are trying to get heard or get others heard. In both sections, I have identified what senior people need to think about. In my view, they have the responsibility (and receive the rewards) for regulating culture. For keeping people safe and noticing who and what is at risk of being marginalised and silenced. A task that should not be delegated but often is.

Finally, it is important to acknowledge this map is incomplete. It is a 'mid-range theory'.[2] It is a guide that offers sufficient detail that the ideas can be tested, evaluated and modified in the light of experience 'back at work'. It is anchored in research and mindful of the effects of context. It is not a comprehensive 'how to' theory that will work in every situation.

Section 1—What to think about before you speak

Thinking about the sort of colleague I want to be

When I stopped thinking it was the heroic few who spoke up, the people around me when I did speak, came into view. If one assumes speaking up is a team effort, time thinking about what sort of colleague I am, you are, can make it more likely I will do or say something helpful. To be a friendly, reliable body alongside you as you speak, to remind you that you are not as alone as you feel. I will be someone who will offer words of encouragement; seek eye contact; and run interference if you're attacked for not being docile and compliant. I will be the person that understands we are all more likely to speak up, go against the grain, if we know we have friends.[3]

I suggest there are three questions we can ask of ourselves and others to have a conversation about how a good colleague behaves and what they sound like.

- ■ *What sort of follower am I?*
- ■ *What sort of bystander am I?*
- ■ *What sort of collaborator am I?*

What sort of follower am I?

Think back to the bed state meeting in Chapter 3. Imagine you are in the meeting. Your attention is drawn to the conversation between Mark and Esther. As if this is the only thing going on. Later, you agree with colleagues that the silencing of Esther was directly attributable to the tone and language of Mark. An attribution that allows you to hold him responsible, and for others to suggest that Esther should just toughen up. The weakness of these sorts of explanations is that it hides, in plain sight—the role of everybody else.

We have to think about followership, in the presence of leadership, because of our propensity to obey and suppress our doubts. As people listened to Mark, some would have felt deeply uncomfortable and said nothing. We need to stop thinking of followership as a quiet compliance. We need to think of our compliance as an offer and always conditional.

If I act as if my cooperation is conditional, I can align my know-how and energy so we can get things done together. I can accept your leadership as long it is possible to talk about the why; for whom; the how; and the what of our approach to the work. If this is silenced, I can withdraw my cooperation because I have another equally important duty. What Caygill[4] calls 'situational resistance'. The duty to try and find a way to speak to who and what is at risk of being silenced. This duty can be self-appointed.

The people I interviewed for my research were provoked to action when they felt their values were at risk of being dismissed by their silence. That what they were really being asked to do was to passively follow the path set by the dominant voices. They remembered they had the right to resist. That they could authorise themselves, because it looked like no one else was going to speak up. They decided they would not join in a diffusion of responsibility, a slide into 'group think'.[5]

The right to resist can be framed as a duty. Enshrined and authorised in the law. This could be organisational policy, or the constitution of a country. The German constitution states (article 20) that all Germans have the 'right to resist any person seeking to abolish this constitutional order, if no other remedy is available'. While not drawing a direct comparison with modern European history, the dynamics that left people silent, complicit and unsafe are not unique to that time. Recent work to understand followership comes back to a characteristic tension.[6] Compliance helps to get things done but, such compliance when coupled with simplistic solutions, tends to result in bad things happening to someone. Usually, those with the least power and those who dissent.

To think about followership, you have to think about how you behave in the presence of leadership. We can behave as if the role of follower is to be passive. History tells us that this makes us all a lot less safe. Better to think of followership as an active role.

My role model for a contingent followership along with Ime (see Chapter 4) is my colleague Dan. He is the archetypal resistor; such is his ability to move unnoticed in the organisation. He picks his moments to challenge. He does not join in collective moaning or get overtly cross or upset. He tends to speak in the quiet moments of a meeting. He might say he is a little troubled before posing an open question. Something like: I notice we are not talking about the way gender determines who is getting heard, are we missing an opportunity here? His skill is to pose an open question and wait. The question is a form of punctuation. To create a pause. An opportunity to collectively clarify, check and develop the meaning we are making as we talk.

In his quiet way, Dan demonstrates that active followership is hard cognitive and emotional work. You have to keep in sight our neurobiological and socialised bias to obedience and conformity. He could resist because he didn't fight every battle.

He knew his values and did not expose himself or weaken his comment, by having it associated with losing emotional control. At its most simple, this kind of contingent followership can be expressed in the statement: *this is what I know and think, I'm interested in what you know about this issue, we will probably make more progress if we work together—what do you think?*

What sort of bystander am I?

Active followership is a struggle and a necessary one if we are not to lapse into by-standing. To be described as such is not to offer a compliment. By-standing is linked to our capacity and willingness to watch and hear others suffer. The failure to shift from empathy to compassion. Katz,[7] arguing that violence against women is a male issue, notes how we are socialised to ignore certain interactions and behaviours. My own experience walking down the footpath and the urinating man, described on p. 46, tells me this is true.

If I can tell myself by-standing is an act of neutrality, this is wrong, it is a decision. At its most risky, it is a form of collaboration with those who would do harm. A form of assistance by not interfering. Not speaking. Not asking any questions about what is going on. Not expressing our doubts about what we see. To being unable or unwilling to use the right words to describe events.[8]

Sailing in the Solent

One of the people I talked to in my research told a really helpful story. She was crewing a yacht in the Solent. They had been racing and were heading back to harbour. The crew were talking and joking. She said she noticed a buoy coming up and wondered if the captain had seen it. It was large so she thought he probably had. She decided to say it anyway and shouted out that there was a buoy to port. Some of the crew laughed. The captain shouted at the crew to stop and thanked her for saying the obvious. He had seen it but was grateful he had her eyes as well.

Her story and subsequent conversation highlighted two things. The role of leadership in mitigating the risks of by-standing and the focus here, on what she described as the 'plonka effect'.

Feeling like a plonka

A 'plonka' is a foolish and inept person. What I worry about as I notice that question in my head, the quickening of my pulse, the churn in my gut, as I contemplate moving from by-standing to trying to and being a good citizen. I tell myself I must have it wrong—but sometimes you have to act the Fool.

Culturally, the Fool is a loyal subject, authorised to check leadership's tendency to hubris.[9] They are like the intermediary discussed in Chapter 1. Conversant in the way of things, never so identified with their desire to belong that they surrender their capacity to think and question. They ask good questions, confront eager compliance, and do not lose their head.

To act the Fool, does not mean I avoid the anxiety of feeling I may actually be stupid. That I am about to get it wrong in public and maybe have my head chopped off. This anxiety has nothing to do with seniority. I have spoken to senior people who tell themselves that they should know this or that by now. As a result, they shut themselves up and miss an opportunity to check if it is just them or is everyone faking it. So, as I worry, I need to try and allow for the possibility that maybe I'm not wrong. If I can allow this question to fully emerge into consciousness then I can then think about what is being asked of me right now.

What sort of collaborator am I?

One aspect of the question – What is being asked of me? – is what becomes possible if I move towards collaboration. 'Collaborator' like 'Fool' is an ambiguous label. A few years ago, I was trying to have a conversation with an activist in Northern Ireland. I asked him how he collaborated with other services. He looked at me and told me I was a ****ing stupid Englishman to use such a term in his presence.

For him, collaboration was another word for collusion with the enemy. This is collaboration as apathy, the absence of resistance. The resigned acceptance that there is nothing I can do. Historically a choice we can face, when subject to overwhelming force.[10] The violent colonisation of one's land, culture and thinking. Subjugation through violence, sometimes state sanctioned and deemed necessary and legal.

At work, we can face another's aggressive assertion of their view of what is right. Another sort of invasion. I was working with the managers of a high-performing team, trying to help them understand why the confidential staff survey reported people feeling bullied. Talking to people privately, they described how the boundary between their public work role and their private 'inner space' was regularly breached. Emails arriving at 11:00 pm and feeling they had to respond. Working when unwell. Taking a call while on holiday. They described feeling like they were occupied by another who insisted their need was greater. As a result, they hid how they felt, to fit in and avoid trouble.

Collaboration is required to be productive. When it leads to a joining of forces, the alignment of interests, sharing the load of changing things. When it happens, it can feel amazing. Listening, talking, being heard, laughing, and doing good work when it becomes hard to know who said what, but all agree it seems to be a good idea.

Because collaboration is ambiguous, it needs constant scrutiny. As I sit around the table, witnessing poor behaviours, in the Friday team meeting, I have to think about what sort of collaborator I am. Is my silence tacit consent? Is it encouragement to those who seek to tell me/us how to think and behave? A consent that hides my fury and resentment, expressed as silence. What can help keep this role in critical sight is an understanding of silence.

Describing the silence

Having words to describe silence is necessary to interpret our own and other's moments of no words, when speaking could be helpful in keeping people safer.[11] There are three types of silence we can employ to express what is in our mind:

- **Acquiescent silence**—there is nothing I can do here.
- **Defensive silence**—I'm too scared to speak.
- **Pro-social silence**—I'm protecting others, so I have to keep quiet.

During a meeting I can monitor my silence (and others) and ask myself what sort of silence is this? Not that one should jump into talking, but to keep checking you have read the situation accurately. Is it really as unsafe as I feel it is? Do I really have nothing to contribute? Is my silence collusive, is someone put at risk? Are we in danger of silencing an important issue?

Silence is not always a conscious choice. We can find ourselves listening to the noise of our inner voice while sitting in silence. We can tell ourselves we are wrong. That we have misunderstood what has been said or implied. We are being too sensitive, and any way they are just stressed. If this is the case, we can begin to loosen the grip of our self-silencing, by thinking about how we can silence ourselves.[12]

- ■ **Judging myself against external standards**—people like me (nurse, woman, junior Dr, etc.) should know this, behave like this. I just need to keep quiet.
- ■ **Putting the needs of others first**—I silence my own desires; they are not as important as yours.
- ■ **Inhibition of self-expression**—people like me do not lose control, I should be nicer, then it will all be ok.
- ■ **A public compliant self and my private emotional self**—inside I'm raging.

Knowing how we can silence ourselves doesn't mean we immediately find our voice. What we do to ourselves has a wider social dimension. As we grow and become adults in the workplace, we take in subtle and not-so-subtle messages about how someone like me (my gender; ethnicity; profession; sexuality; class) should talk to whom, about what, with what voice and language. Being black or non-binary can feel wrong in the face of the silent assumption of whiteness and heterosexuality. So, we also have to hear silence as the way of the powerful. As a white, European male the world is pretty much as I like it. I can sit in silence because not much is going to change around here. So, I do not need to enter the conversation.[13]

What sort of leader am I?

The Fool is a necessary role, authorised by the court, to take up the role of a loyal doubter, to guard against the hubristic leader. Hubris is a blustering, dangerous parody of thoughtful leadership.[14] As such, I am overconfident in my abilities; that it will all go well; I aggressively silence any voice that does not mirror and affirm my way of thinking and behaving. I am a leader who thrives on the acquiescent silence of my followers.

Leaders need confidence but it does not require them to hide their questions and anxieties about what is going on and what to do. Sometimes the way forward is making the right choice from an established set of actions. The situation may be complicated but if we choose right, there should not be too much uncertainty. Leadership is also about facing up to situations that are hard to define, are complex. Therefore, it is hard to decide what will work, and whatever we do, there will be unintended consequences that will need noticing and our attention. We will need to work together. This requires a sense that regardless of rank and status I will be heard, it is safe enough to speak.

Psychological safety—what good leaders help establish

The best leaders I have known took seriously their duty to try and create the conditions for people to talk, inquire, argue; agree if that felt right; and question any agreement if it were anchored in the avoidance of doubt and difference.[15] That good leadership was not to be measured in agreement but in inquiry[16] and a willingness to keep asking—why do we believe this to be the case? To do this requires a sense of psychological safety. That is:

> *The belief that the work environment is safe for inter-personal risk taking. The concept refers to the feeling of being able speak up with relevant ideas, questions, or concerns. Psychological safety is present when colleagues trust and respect each other and feel able— even obligated—to be candid.*[17]

Defining it, talking about it is not the same as having it. Psychological safety; compassionate leadership; servant leadership are concepts I have heard championed as if already in play. This is using ideas, anchored in listening to avoid a more interesting question. *How do we do this, in the face of relentless pressure and a regulatory framework (the rules, constraints, requirements of our 'industry') that can be hard to satisfy?* To ask this question is an act of leadership, anchored in humility, not hubris. The following can help explore this question.

- Explicitly asking to hear different ideas based on experience, profession, and background. To invite people to offer their best thinking based on what is currently known.
- Asking people to critique current thinking and when they do, not responding too defensively. That is, modelling the skill and desirability of lowering one's defences and resistance to questioning.
- Acknowledging and apologising if one does react defensively and talking about the challenge of hearing one's hard-won thoughts and plans questioned. Doing this to encourage people that there is an argumentation culture around here. That doubt and questioning are core leadership skills, required of everyone.
- Intervening when people seek to shut others up. Asking, why is this necessary and why now?
- Noticing who or what is silent in the conversation, that may be evidence of self-silencing. Restating the invitation to speak. Asking, who or what are we avoiding by our silence?

A final comment about leadership in this section is about following the rules. I have worked with people who ask the right questions and who can opt out when it suits them to stop following the rules. It is an interesting behaviour. It is exciting to work with people who are mavericks. It is also a behaviour that raises a question about the use of power. If I am the most senior person in the room, I can justify my actions because of my status. The rules and norms are there to constrain this power. If I knowingly disregard these, I am letting people know that I am above these. This does not help in terms of my duty to develop a sense of psychological safety. My followers need to keep in mind the good of my leadership.

Leadership is not always for the good

As a leader and a follower, I can lapse into the assumption that leadership is for the good. Such a belief enables me to find common cause and collaborate. It also risks that I become a docile follower. I stop thinking about our joint purpose and stop testing this against my own values.

Most definitions of leadership emphasise skills, not outcomes. Effective leaders enable, adapt, cooperate, prioritise, make sense of things, offer a vision. Good leadership can lead to bad things happening. History is replete with people who have argued a plausible common purpose, to face a moment of exception, such that the 'old ways' and the rule of law can be ignored.

Keeping the assumed good of leadership and followership in critical sight is helped if we can use the right words to describe those forms of leadership, we may wish to pretend we will never do or come across. Kellerman[18] in her book, Bad Leadership, offers a useful language to evaluate if we are in the presence of bad leadership and if we are in danger of enabling this.

- **Incompetent**—I lack the know-how to do what is required.
- **Rigid**—I refuse to go beyond what I know even if what I know is insufficient for the challenges we face.
- **Intemperate**—I fail to control my emotions.
- **Callous**—I am indifferent to the needs of others.
- **Insular**—I am not interested in anyone outside of my group who I owe a duty of care to.
- **Corrupt**—my interests always come before yours and what is right.
- **Evil**—I use harm and terror to achieve my purpose.

Another important question

A sense of psychological safety means I can think. Thinking is a form of resistance, in the face of the pressure to be quiet and compliant. I can think about my followership and collaborative style. I can think about how I am behaving and why. I can think about alternatives, I can remind myself I have agency. I can also think about how others are behaving and how this determines our culture. If I am to avoid a passive followership, I also need to think about what sort of organisation or community am I part of.[19] I can ask the following questions:

- What have I agreed to become a part of?
- What attracts me to this group, organisation, community?
- What are my concerns about how we speak to each other?
- What are we ignoring and silencing?
- What have I forgotten since I joined?
- Where are the gaps between our espoused values and what we do?
- Where are my red lines?

These questions can be asked in the privacy of my own thinking or out loud. However we ask them, they can help keep the everyday culture we are part of in critical view. Asking them out loud will provide even more data and offer a clue about what sort of leadership and followership one is in the presence of.

The effects of bullying and incivility are real

The intention of behaviour can always be contested. I didn't mean to be rude; you're just too sensitive. What you hear as aggressive, I see as clarity in a tight spot. I don't say good morning to you, I'm too busy.

A way to 'lift' the conversation out of the subjective, is to define basic behaviours using descriptions from the more objective research literature into poor behaviour in organisations and teams. A degree of objectivity means one can step back from the interpersonal domain of these behaviours. To think about why these behaviours may erupt to manage some organisational or system issue, as described in Chapter 2 and the bed state meeting.

A basic terminology

Rudeness is insensitive or disrespectful behaviour, enacted by a person who has little or no regard for others.[20]

Incivility is low-intensity rudeness or unsociable behaviour/speech that occurs with ambiguous intention to harm, lacking regard for others and in violation of workplace norms.[21]

Bullying is an ongoing and deliberate misuse of power in relationships through repeated verbal, physical and/or social behaviour that intends to cause physical, social and/or psychological harm. It can involve an individual or a group misusing their power, or perceived power, over one or more persons who feel unable to stop it from happening.[22]

These behaviours land differently for different people. If I am part of a group(s) that is already marginalised, who feel less psychological safety, feel I lack agency, the impact of these behaviours will be more profound. What may be a 'moment' for me, will be just one more, never-ending reminder of one's place for someone else. Where defensive silence is a rational response to threat.[23]

Understand the effects

My reaction to being ignored, shouted at, can be dismissed by me and others, as a sign of my weakness, my sensitivity. As if anyone else experiencing the same behaviour would be fine. The research shows this to be an invalid explanation. Most of us respond in the ways noted below.[24]

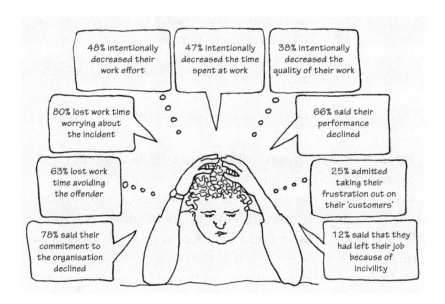

While these responses are described in relation to incivility, I would argue they apply to all three dimensions of intemperate behaviour. If the outcomes noted above are valid, then our response cannot be easily dismissed. Embedded in these effects is a question about the cost of these behaviours. A fact that should be a concern to any leader, any board, any director of finance. The loss of the most valuable resource in any team or organisation—people's capacity to think and collaborate. Little attention is paid to these losses.

The shouter, the bully, the rude, all rob the team or organisation of what helps it 'work'. If they were stealing the photocopier, you would expect action. It's tangible. The research shows that cognitive loss is also tangible. Within the NHS the annual cost of these behaviours is estimated to be £2.281 billion.[25]

It is also the case that being a witness to these behaviours has a similar effect. People decrease work commitment; become less collaborative; feel emotionally depleted; and are preoccupied with the 'event'.[26]

It's not just personal

While it feels personal to be silenced and silent, hope lies in assuming that it's more than this. Hope that we are not lacking, wrong, or deviant, but that we have stumbled upon or pointed to an issue in the wider system. An issue that can evoke dread, anxiety or shame if it were to surface in the conversation. Something discomforting that is best forced back below the surface. If this is the case, two questions can be asked.

- *Am I the only one thinking and feeling like something needs to be said?*
- *If this attack upon me is not just because I deserve it, what is the issue that is being silenced? What is my hunch, my best guess?*

Question one can help build that sense of authority to speak. If I am not alone maybe I will hear some support. Question two similarly builds momentum. If it is not just me and about me, what is required of me, given my role, profession and expertise? How do I make a useful contribution as we grapple with this messy issue in this room today? The next section explores what to think about and do in these sorts of moments.

Section 2—In the moment

Not everything can be anticipated. Having a language to describe followership, bad leadership etc. can alert one to some of the risks; and in the end you have got to try and change things. This means stepping into a degree of uncertainty. Aspects of this were explored in the second version of stories, told in Chapters 2 to 5. The aim of these versions was to keep it real. Modest interventions that do not require heroic or perfect execution and a receptive audience. What follows here are some pointers when you have to think in the moment. When you cannot, will not sit there in docile silence. When you answer the question—what is being asked of me in this situation? When you want to shift the conversation, to find out more about what is going on as we struggle with this issue, on a wet Wednesday afternoon and we are all exhausted.

Ask good questions

A way to increase the possibility of speaking, in what can feel like an uncertain or hostile environment, is to ask an open question. The sort of question that seeks to probe what is going on without disclosing too much of one's own thinking/feeling. A question that invites the recipient to say more. These questions can work.[27]

1. If we had a greater sense of psychological safety, what would we talk about and who would benefit?
2. Can you say something more about what leads you to assume/think/believe this to be the case? I want to understand.
3. What prevents you/us from bringing this (difficult) issue up?
4. What would make it safer to talk this through?
5. What makes us so sure about this intervention/way of thinking? It's a really complex issue.
6. What am I/we not understanding?

7. Where are we/you less certain about this intervention/ way of thinking?
8. Who or what is missing from our conversation?
9. What could we be turning a deaf ear, blind eye to as we talk about this issue?
10. When are we at our best, so not like this?

These questions draw people out and build the psychological safety that is required if they are to be answered. Think about the times you have been on the receiving end of someone who tells you what is going on and what you should do. It can feel parental. You can either accept or question their advice. Either way it is hard to talk about your sense of what is going on, to explore possibilities. Open questions are a way to make explicit and concrete any commitment to diversity of thought. A way to help people learn when already learned; when what is known is insufficient for the challenges we now face.[28]

Finally, a good question is more potent, when after it has been quietly uttered, someone says—*that's a good question, let's take a moment to think about it.*

My imposter voice—accepting the burden of my competence

Bullying and incivility can erupt to contain the risk of a thought forcing its way into the public domain. That what we know is insufficient for the challenges we now face. In Chapter 2, Mark is unable to consider the possibility there may be a better way to manage the pressure he and the group face. He and others may think he is resolving matters by being firm and decisive. Telling Esther to JFD is symptomatic of a hubristic leadership. A leadership that silences dissent and frames the safety issues articulated by Esther as a 'no go' area.

Such a leadership imposes a docile followership, mindless collaboration. Understanding these possibilities and having a stock of good questions can help resist being a bystander. What can also help is accepting the burden of one's competence. If I feel like a fake, an imposter, despite repeated success, I carry the burden of my imagined chronic inadequacy.[29] This doesn't extinguish my competence, it just makes it hard to accept it, feel secure in it, to act from it. A lack of personal confidence can be amplified by our willingness to defer to the confident.[30] Sometimes this is warranted. Sometimes it is a person who has an excessively high opinion of their abilities; saying they know best; and then making the unwarranted claim they are right. History tells us these people are attractive and a disaster, when paired with a docile followership.

Add to this the tendency of men to be the ones who overestimate their know-how, and for women to do the opposite; the opportunity to do the wrong thing collectively and confidently is a risk.[31] A risk that is mitigated if we can push through our lack of confidence and turn up. As Jess Philips bluntly points out:

> 'The world is run by those who show up. Don't assume you can't be one of those people or that you don't have the skills or fancy language to do it'.[32]

Feeling like an imposter is a reason we can give ourselves for not showing up. The following is based on my conversations with people who were constructively awkward. People who found a way to speak (sometimes). These ideas can tip the balance towards our competence; our know-how; our insight; our intelligence.

1. **Assume you may not be wrong**—question the assumption that you are. Has that always been the case? And if

you are wrong, what is likely to happen? What could you say or do to mitigate any bad consequences?

2. **Listen to the voice(s) in your head**—this is how we consider what is being asked of us in a situation. Give it space and volume and remember you are under no obligation to speak out loud or be heroic. Think about what feels like the least risky thing to say. Think about what it might feel like to stay quiet.

3. **Assume you're not the only one**—as discussed, silence is not necessarily agreement. It is easy to assume everyone else is sitting there getting it; and you're the only stupid one. This is unlikely to be true, particularly if the situation under consideration is complex.

4. **Be guided by your feelings**—anger; outrage; confusion can tell us what is important to us. An assumption that excludes certain people or groups; a sharp word; a put-down, may trigger strong feelings. They do not have to be acted on but recognised as a signal that something important to us is at risk of being ignored.

5. **Bring your values to work**—what's important to us in our lives outside work will be important in work. If I think being respectful is important, I will notice a lack of respect at work. It will evoke feelings and remind me that this thing is important to me and that I face a choice. Silence or finding a way to say something.

6. **Not be overly agreement seeking**—I can behave as if 'getting along' is our shared task. While actively seeking not to do so disrupts cooperation in a team or group, suppressing differences can slide us into 'group think'.[33] A lack of diversity about what we think and how we think together. It can be useful to think that one has a responsibility to argue—not to compete with or destroy the person but to evaluate ideas and seek alternatives. To ask questions. To question what is taken to be right and proper around here.[34]

7. **Think 'both and'**—the drive toward agreement can reduce the options, exclude alternatives and a tacit acceptance that our resulting intervention may leave some people, groups or issues out. Thinking both/and is to refuse to forget that as we solve this issue over here; there will be consequences over there. For example, we have cleared the emergency department and now we now need to think about who is where and if they are safe enough. The question is—*who or what are we at risk of forgetting and could I make it safer if I say something about that?*

8. **Be the best prepared in the room**—what helped the people I spoke to, tackle say an issue like racism in a meeting, was to feel the confidence of having read the papers. Understanding the data helped them notice how it was being used in the meeting to build an invalid theory, for example, about the attainment of young black children in school. Reading the papers; noticing who or what is missing from the agenda, is work that can be done prior to as well as during a meeting/conversation.

9. **It just needs to be good enough**—there is nothing more dispiriting and silencing than holding oneself to an impossible standard. Speaking up, in the middle of a fractious meeting will not go perfectly. We will feel anxious as we anticipate all that could go wrong. We may freeze, a normal response to feeling overwhelmed and having insufficient time to process what is going on. However, if I wait until I have constructed the perfect intervention in my head, the moment may pass. Good enough is all that is required. This means turning down the volume on that voice in our heads that requires us to be perfect and saying to yourself, right or wrong I have to try and say this. . . .

10. **Be a good colleague**—speaking up is a team effort. If you cannot say it this time, be ready to nod approval or back up whoever does find a way to speak; and if you're the boss, be kind.

Compassion, not empathy

Empathy is being able to imagine how another person may be feeling. Our willingness to notice and feel another's pain. I can do this silently in my head. I can reach out to you after a meeting and say I'm sorry that it was so hard for you. It is an important gesture that can be self-serving. I see your pain but I am not going to intervene this time.

Thinking back to Carole in Chapter 3. Her comment was meant as consoling, an expression of empathy—*the patient would have died anyway.* It can be an intervention we reach for when what we actually want to do is close down the conversation. When we want to sustain the belief that kind and empathic attention has been expressed, even if it is really hard to feel it. We can guess when Carole sees Jane, she is already feeling overloaded by work. It makes it less likely she can stop long enough to understand Jane's situation. This kind of nod and walk by is understandable in their high-demand, scary jobs.

We can also guess that Carole is trying to manage the dilemma of empathy. Carole is an experienced surgeon. She will have her own memories of things going badly. Such memories enable her to recognise Jane's distress. As she reaches out to Jane, she can become aware of her own experiences lurking below her conscious awareness. She really understands the mess and the loneliness of being abandoned to these memories by others' silence. Her brief intervention expresses the understandable and natural wish not to think about the people she has lost.

Carole can be said to fail in her leadership task. She fails to move from empathy to compassion. Compassion being the move from 'I notice your pain, feel your pain' to, 'I will now intervene to try and help'. This move is really hard when you (like Carole) are already overloaded by work, stressed, flooded with glucocorticoids, hungry or thirsty. In such a state my own heart is probably thumping louder than yours. As such I must prioritise my need to keep myself safe. I can access my capacity for empathy when I hear your heart over the pounding in my own chest.[35]

Compassion is a form of practical kindness because it seeks to address the cause, not the symptom. This means it can also be tough to say and receive. My supervisor (see pages 44–45) exemplified compassion. He could have just gone along with how I said I felt. This would have been empathy and not enough. A passive intervention, just going along with things. He understood that how I was thinking about my situation was the problem. My anxiety was a symptom, not the cause of my distress. Having my hand held and told it would all be ok would have been to elevate my symptom to the status of the problem that needed sorting. Put another way, I am looking up the face of a climb. Of course, I'm anxious. I'm scared of heights and I want to get to the top. We could spend hours trying to reason my anxiety away but what will really help is being taught how to use a rope, pitons, and to work with my climbing partners. I might feel better for a while. However, the underlying issue, how I authorised myself, in this new longed-for role would remain unexplored, unresolved.

There are reasons we are not moved to compassion. Our own exhaustion; a worry that our own memories and pain will surface; a worry we will get it wrong and look and sound stupid. A few things can help.

1. **Practice**—builds confidence, it can reduce the scenario planning we do in our heads as we rehearse an intervention. The line of thought that delays things until the moment has passed.
2. **Self-assessment**—what sort of intervention is this?
   a. Is my intervention limited to empathy?
   b. What is stopping me from speaking to what I think is really required here?

   c. What is being asked of me in this situation?

   d. What should a person with my knowledge and authority do?

   e. What can I do to help others who are trying to draw attention to the underlying issues here?

3. **Look after yourself**—a lack of food, poor hydration can affect cognition and decision making.[36] Resist the normalisation of missed breaks and when that is impossible be kind to yourself when you choose safety over a risky intervention.

Think about the job

The demands of the day-to-day work readily fall into silence. They are taken for granted. Something we learn not to talk about. When I was talking with Jane about her experience in theatre, it struck me how strange it is to have a job that confronts you with blood and bodies every day.[37] Opening people up, putting them to sleep. Taking this responsibility, shouldering the blame if it goes wrong. Then going home to look after the children.

Not talking about the job is part of the web of strategies professionals adopt and are inducted into, to help do the work. A form of healthy denial, a way of sustaining the objectivity required to keep focused on a greater good. As I trained to be a nurse, I was hardly aware that a quiet part of the curriculum was to learn how to suppress and then ignore my everyday response to my fear and disgust, so I could do my job. Clean up faeces; take a punch to the head; face down an angry person. The downside of this capability was that it became harder to notice and talk about the incremental impact of these experiences.

I eventually felt overwhelmed but lacked the words to talk about this. Our managers did try and help. I remember sitting in the weekly support group, led by a kind, well-known, therapist. Bewilderment and silence are the words that capture my experience. Also, a sense of possibility and frustration. What was missing were the words to talk about what we were experiencing. Without words it was impossible to talk and see if this was a shared experience and to see how our culture was helping to keep people safer or not.[38] Of course, a psychodynamic approach is really helpful but it requires time, which we did not have. It felt like being out of your depth in a rough sea; the rescue boat turns up and instead of being heaved aboard, the person leans over and patiently starts to teach you how to swim.

The lack of words, the lack of a leadership, willing and able to sanction and model this sort of inquiry-based conversation left us isolated and silent. Questions about how we thought and behaved, the balance between therapy and containment, compassion and indifference did not get asked. As if asking these questions, exploring these possibilities, were not part of our work as professionals.

If we agree to forget the nature of the work and its impact on us, we enter a collusive silence. This allows us to do difficult work, which others would find hard. It can also lead to an excessive strain on individuals, amplified by not having a language to talk about it and a culture that if you do, can be heard as a lack of professionalism.[39]

It is safer to accept that the work has emotional consequences. That the way work is described and organised can help to contain anxiety, so the job can be done. Such containment can make it almost impossible to talk about these feelings, without losing face. The following can help and the burden of offering such help falls mainly to senior leaders.

1. *What do I do to acknowledge and remind people that the work has emotional impact and it can overwhelm people's capacity to work and speak in certain contexts?*

2. *How do I evaluate and sustain sufficient psychological safety around here?*
3. *What do I do to question the assumption that being overwhelmed is a matter of personal weakness and nothing to do with the way we organise work?*
4. *What do I do to narrow the gap between what I imagine people do and their lived experience of work?*
5. *How do I talk about my own lived experience?*

Conclusion

I have ended this guide with a list of things to try. Some stuff may be useful, but it is based on other people's experiences. Try and build your own understanding of how you can be silenced; resist being silenced; and find your voice. How you learnt to be good; quiet; argumentative and questioning as you grew; got educated; then joined a profession or organisation. This self-knowledge can help us remember how we find ourselves; hesitating to speak in the team meeting is not all we can be and do. There is just something about this meeting. Practice seems to help, as well as accepting that it may not go as we would wish. But if our intention is good and we have good colleagues we will probably be ok.

Notes

1 Macfarlane, R. (2008) *Mountains of the mind*. London: Grant. (p. 184).
2 It lies, according to Merton (1968) quoted in Pawson and Tilley,

> 'Between the minor but necessary working hypotheses that evolve in abundance during day-to-day

research and the all-inclusive systematic efforts to develop a unified theory that will explain all the observed uniformities of social behaviour, social organization and social change'.

(Pawson and Tilley, 1997, p. 123)

Pawson, R. and Tilley, N. (1997) *Realistic evaluation*. London: Sage.

3 In the final chapter of her book, Sanderson talks about finding a friend:

> 'For those of us who aren't naturally moral rebels, finding a like-minded friend to stand by our side can be an essential step toward giving us the ability to show moral courage'.
>
> (p. 206)

Sanderson, C. (2020) *The Bystander effect. The psychology of courage and inaction*. London: William Collins.

4 Caygill, H. (2013) *On resistance. A philosophy of defiance*. London: Bloomsbury.

5 Latane, B. and Darley, J. (1968) Group inhibition of bystander intervention in emergencies. *Journal of Personality and Social Psychology*, 10(3), pp. 215–221.

6 See Kellerman, B. (2004) *Bad leadership. What it's, how it happens, why it matters*. Boston: Harvard Business School Press.

> 'Should followers follow the leader, or the dictates of their consciences? On the one hand, a strong argument can be made that to maintain order and get work done, followers should go along with the leader except in dire circumstances. On the other hand, followers are not sheep, nor should they necessarily be part of any herd'.
>
> (Kellerman, 2004, p. 30)

7 Katz, J. (2019) *The macho paradox. Why some men hurt women and how all men can help*. Naperville: Sourcebooks.

8 Cohen, S. (2001) *States of denial. Knowing about atrocities and suffering*. Cambridge: Polity.

> 'Denial in the sense of shutting out the awareness of other's suffering—is the normal state of affairs. This

> *is precisely why so much effort has to be devoted to breaking out of this frame. Far from being pushed into accepting reality, people have to be dragged out of reality'.*
>
> (p. 247)

9 'The jester is privileged in that, under the guise of madness or stupidity (which suggest harmlessness), he can iterate the otherwise unspeakable . . . The sage/fool is often the only person who can protect the king from hubris' (Kets De Vries, 2003, p. 63).

Kets de Vries, M. (2003) *Leaders, fools and impostors.* Lincoln: iUniverse.

10 See Morgan, P. (2018) *Hitlers collaborators. Choosing between bad and worse in Nazi—occupied Western Europe.* Oxford: Oxford University Press.

11 Van Dyne, L., Ang, S. and Botero, C. (2003) Conceptualizing employee silence and employee voice as multidimensional constructs. *Journal of Management Studies*, 40(6), September, pp. 1359–1392.

12 Jack, D. (1991) *Silencing the self. Women and depression.* London: Harvard University Press.

13 Macalpine, M. and Marsh, S. (2005) 'On being white: There is nothing I can say'. Exploring whiteness and power in organisations. *Management Learning*, 36(4), pp. 429–450.

14 Sadler-Smith, E. (2019) *Hubristic leadership.* London: Sage.

15 See Kramer, E.-H. (2007) *Organizing doubt. Grounded theory, army units and dealing with dynamic complexity.* Oxford: Liber and Copenhagen Business Press.

16 Appiah, K. (2006) *Cosmopolitanism. Ethics in a world of strangers.* London: Allen Lane.

> *'Understanding one another may be hard; it can certainly be interesting. But it does not require that we come to agreement'*
>
> (p. 78).

17 Edmondson, A. (2019) *The fearless organisation. Creating psychological safety in the workplace for learning, innovation, and growth.* Hoboken, NJ: Wiley, p. 8.

18 Kellerman, B. (2004) *Bad leadership. What it is, how it happens, why it matter.* Boston: Harvard Business School, pp. 38–46.

19 McKie, A. (2004) 'The demolition of man': Lessons from Holocaust literature for the teaching of nursing ethics. *Nursing Ethics*, 11(2), pp. 138–149, 140.

20 Porath, C. and Erez, A. (2007) Does rudeness matter? The effects of rudeness on task performance and helpfulness. *Academy of Management Journal*, 50(5), pp. 1181–1197.

21 Cortina, L., Leskinen, M. and Magley, V. (2011) Selective incivility as modern discrimination in organisations: Evidence and impact. *Journal of Management*, 39(6), pp. 1579–1605.

22 www.ncab.org.au/bullying-advice/bullying-for-parents/definition-of-bullying/

23 The percentage of BME and white staff experiencing harassment, bullying or abuse from staff in the last 12 months has been increasing since 2016.

For all trust types, a higher percentage of BME staff experienced harassment, bullying or abuse from staff in the last 12 months compared to white staff.

NHS (2019) *Workforce race equality standard 2019 report—2019 data analysis report for NHS trusts* [Online]. Available from: www.england.nhs.uk/wp-content/uploads/2020/01/wres-2019-data-report.pdf (Accessed: 25th August 2021).

Berdahl, J. and Moore, C. (2006) Workplace harassment: Double jeopardy for minority women. *Journal of Applied Psychology*, 91(2), pp. 426–436.

24 Porath, C. (2016) The hidden toll of workplace incivility. *McKinsey Quarterly* [online]. Available from: www.mckinsey.com/business-functions/organization/our-insights/the-hidden-toll-of-workplace-incivility?cid=eml-web (Accessed: 30th December 2021).

25 Kline, R. and Lewis, D. (2018) The price of fear: Estimating the financial cost of bullying and harassment to the NHS in England. *Public Policy and Management*, 39(3), pp. 166–174.

26 Porath, C. and Erez, A. (2009) Overlooked but not untouched; how rudeness reduces onlookers' performance on routine creative tasks. *Organisational Behaviour and Human Decision Processes*, 109, pp. 29–44.

27 Based on: Kleiner, A. (2008) *The age of heretics*. San Francisco: Jossey-Bass.

28 Argyris, C. (1991) Teaching smart people to learn. *Harvard Business Review*, 69(3), May–June, pp. 99–109.

29 Clance, P.R. and Imes, S. (1978) The impostor phenomenon in high achieving women: Dynamics and therapeutic intervention. *Psychotherapy: Theory, Research and Practice*, 15, pp. 241–247.

30 Olah, N. (2019) Imposter syndrome? It's a matter of class, not health. *The Guardian*, 17th October (Opinion section), p. 4.

31 Sieghart, M. (2021) *The authority gap*. London: Penguin Random House.

32 Philips, J. (2019) *Truth to power. 7 ways to call time on B.S.* London: Monoray. (p. 212).

33 Janis, I. and Mann, L. (1997) *Decision making. A psychological analysis of conflict, choice and commitment*. London: Macmillan.

34 Kramer, E.-H. (2007) *Organizing doubt. Grounded theory, army units and dealing with dynamic complexity*. Oxford: Liber and Copenhagen Business Press.

35 Sapolsky, R. (2017) *Behave. The biology of humans at our best and worst*. London: Vintage. (p. 543).

36 Danziger, S., Levav, J. and Avnaim-Pesso, L. (2011) Extraneous factors in judicial decisions. *Proceedings of the National Academy of Sciences*, 108, pp. 6889–6892.

37 Winnicott, D.W. (1947) Hate in the countertransference. *International Journal of Psychoanalysis*, 30, pp. 69–74.

    Winnicott recognises and validates the possibility of hatred in the work of caring. He does not condemn or imagine it can be banished. The ethical task is to notice how such feeling can be aroused by 'the heavy emotional burden on those who care' (p. 194). Not to face this emotion is to risk doing harm.

38 See Elton, C. (2018) *Also human. The inner lives of doctors*. London: Heinemann.

39 Menzies, L.I. (1988) *Containing anxiety in institutions*. London: Free Association Books.

Chapter 7

Can we talk about our conversational culture?

Introduction

This chapter picks up a thread first seen in Chapter 1. How a person with no heroic intentions answers that simple but challenging question—*what is being asked of me right now as I sit with my team in this meeting?* A meeting where I am not the most senior or junior person present. Where we have known each other for a while and I think, with a degree of confidence, I am respected and valued. For my work and commitment to trying to do the right thing. The sort of person others want to talk to when things do not go so well in the meeting. When a conversation in the café is needed to de-brief, have a moan, rehearse what would have been said if people could have spoken.

What if, after one of these conversations, we think maybe we need to take all this, whatever it is, back into our meeting? Rather than dealing with 'it' by blowing off some steam outside. What can we do? What follows are ideas, in the form of notes, to make the case that it can be useful to slow down, in our taken for granted, everyday way of talking as a team. To pause and think about that which determines so much of how we work—the conversational culture we have developed. A culture that is really hard to see and hear. These notes can be used as the basis of something formal, when you are trying to influence senior people, or informally, with your peers. These ideas are not an exercise in 'soft skills', but a way to investigate an aspect of the everyday that is usually hidden. Therefore, not soft but rational, thoughtful and confronting. Things that can get hidden are usually banished for a reason. Rediscovering why that might be can keep people safer, make work more efficient but also may make people anxious. For example:

The policy meeting

The safety team has come together to review the various guidance offered for people at risk of sepsis, falling and rapid deterioration. Basically, anything bad that can happen to you, this team will know what others should be doing. The meeting is full of yet more ideas about keeping people safer. You cannot argue the good intentions or the evidence supporting the guidance. A brave person, a ward manager, asked a question. I paraphrase (she hedged her basic observation with a lot of thanks for the guidance)—if this guidance is so good why do the incident rates remain so high?

This was not what people wanted to hear. A member of the team laughed. Later, she explained that the look on everyone's faces was a joy. The outrage followed by a flash of recognition that good policy was conflated with effective application and behaviour change. That in reality, the challenge of application across multiple contexts had been silenced. Except that when policy was not followed, the experts just shouted louder that people should follow the policy.

This meeting was not exceptional and the people who gathered were clever and wanted to make a difference. While they did not welcome the comment, they recognised it drew their attention to something they had mostly ignored. It led them to spending time trying to understand the different contexts their work was trying to influence. To understanding, however good the policy is, it is always taken up in different and surprising ways. The gap between work as imagined and prescribed; and as experienced and disclosed. Better to know this complexity and work with it, then pretend it is simple.

What follows is a set of notes developed from watching and talking to people I have worked with. People who know something about creating pauses in the teams they are a part of. Teams in which they cannot invoke positional or coercive powers to get people to stop. People, whose practical know-how can encourage colleagues to slow it down; to think about how their group or team is 'doing' its talking. People who recognise how the language and familiar process of the meeting may direct attention to certain issues and away from others.

People who argue that everyone is a bit safer if, periodically, we look at where the fences are. The markers that separate what we take for granted and what we tend to ignore; and that sometimes it is right to pull a few fences down.

To note

While these notes include material drawn from the bullying and incivility literature, I am assuming the context is not so explicit. If it is, go to Chapter 8. This will offer you a step-by-step guide to address these issues. For example, where unprofessional behaviours are being reported to HR and in staff surveys. I am assuming here that things are generally going ok but there is an interest in exploring what is enabling and disrupting our work around here, by noticing a bit more of what is going below the surface.

Making the case—Part 1

If this work were a game, then this section is about warming up. Exploring ideas with the leadership. To negotiate the authority to act and work through any initial reluctance to stop and think and ask the substantive question:

> *Is the way we talk to each other the best we can do to keep people safer and to work efficiently together and with others?*

Why do we need to stop and think?

It can be a challenge to ask people to take seriously the idea that thinking about their talking, is a useful thing to do. It can feel like an unaffordable luxury in a busy work setting. What can help is a drawing a distinction between two types of talking.

Making a distinction in how we talk

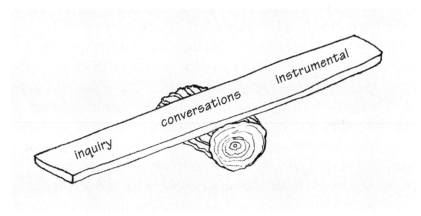

We take how we talk, the language and tone we use, for granted. We think of our talking as instrumental. It is talk as telling. It is how to get things done. As long as they do and things get done, why worry? Work is busy enough and we should not assume such talk is in any way wrong. It has its place.

A reason to stop and ask the substantive question is that instrumental talking works ok when the task is clear and there is a correct intervention. We just need to execute it well. It is a less useful approach when what the team actually faces is complexity. When it is hard to pin down the challenge and what a good solution looks like. When whatever you decide to do, triggers unforeseen consequences that will need managing. The bed state meeting described in Chapter 3 is an example of this sort of complexity.

When a team faces complexity, there are two requirements. To resist pretending it is just complicated and try to create an environment conducive to inquiry and learning.

In the policy meeting example above, the complexity of the task—how you help people change behaviour in different contexts—was suppressed. Policy just needs to be clear and we tell people to apply it consistently and correctly. If they do not, they are the problem and need to be dealt with accordingly. The intervention of the ward manager and the laughter of the team member, in recognition of a point well made, had the potential to shift the meeting out of its instrumental mindset to one conducive to inquiry. So, rather than see policy failure as ultimately a disciplinary issue, it led to the team trying to understand it as a symptom of something interesting. Something they had not thought about; something to explore whilst not being preoccupied with quick solutions. The team realising that trying to do the same thing better, will not achieve the outcome of keeping people safer. What is required is to inquire and so to learn. To learn about the gap between what we know and what we want to achieve; to bear the anxiety as we wait to learn new things; and then feel competent again, as we integrate our new know-how.

Let's not assume learning is easy

The people who have to (and want to) respond to inquiries into service failure understandably respond with the intention to learn from events. Learning from events means we have to question what we know. This is hard cognitive and emotional work. The sort of work we may choose to avoid, so condemning ourselves to repeating the same mistakes. Why else do these reports sound so repetitive? One reason is the learning required, after systemic failure, is not easy and this is not acknowledged.

The requirement to learn and the intention to learn is insufficient, when not coupled to an understanding and tolerance of the difficulty of learning. Learning is a challenge, especially when I think of myself as already qualified and learned.[1] A self-assessment of competence that, based on the people I work with, is accurate and a trap. A trap because I can be understandably reluctant to step outside of my 'knowing'; to investigate, evaluate, discuss and change some of the deeper assumptions that underpin how I and we do things around here.

To inquire into what is taken for granted requires courage and encouragement because it is to risk feeling incompetent and sounding stupid. What Ed Schein calls 'learning anxiety'.[2] To face this can be a tough task if you are senior, experienced and the person others come to when they are uncertain. It is understandable if we sometimes act to resist learning as a way to conserve our sense of ourselves as competent. However, to do this risks superficiality in translating the hard-won insights, into what has gone wrong or could be improved, into practical action.

We have to take care to create the conditions for people to feel safe enough to do the learning that is fundamental to inquiry-based conversations.

The trouble with learning and what helps...

Learning anxiety

The worry I will look and sound incompetent as I learn new things and before they are integrated into my know how.

Schein, E. (2013) *Humble inquiry. The gentle art of asking instead of telling* San Francisco: Berrett-Koehler.

Establish psychological safety

'The belief that the work environment is safe for interpersonal risk taking. The concept refers to the feeling of being able speak up with relevant ideas, questions, or concerns. Psychological safety is present when colleagues trust and respect each other and feel able – even obligated- to be candid' (p.8).

Edmonson, A. (2019) *The fearless organisation. Creating psychological safety in the workplace for learning, innovation, and growth.* New Jersey: Wiley.

There is no point framing learning anxiety as 'only' resistance. As if one is exercising a choice not to learn. The kinder and tougher message is to acknowledge it and confront any ridicule of less than perfect new behaviours. To create a culture where such risk-taking is the mark of an effective leader; the behaviour of the professionally competent; the person who is not surprised that all they know is insufficient for some of the challenges they and the team face.

One last thing can help. To temporarily separate out the normal (instrumental) business meetings of the team or group and the inquiry work. This allows for a conversation about ground rules to make an inquiry conversation safer. Normally, in day-to-day meetings, it is assumed anybody can talk about what anybody else has said and how they have said it. It is not seen as privileged. It can help to build the sense of psychological safety, during the awkward learning phase, to discuss and agree some basic rules. For example:

	What we say and how we say it, is not to be shared outside of this conversation, unless we agree.
	We practice forgiveness – some of what we say and how we say it will be clumsy.
Making it safer to learn...	We have the right to change our minds, think outloud and express our thoughts and feelings.
	We have a duty to think together and be curious, even if I think you are wrong, misguided, ill-informed.
	While I think I am right, I accept the possibility I may not be and we are ok with that.
	We always bring our conversation back to the question - *is the way we talk to each other the best we can do to keep people safer and to work efficiently together and with others?*

If the above is to help people think about how they need to have the conversation, the next section suggests what to think about to begin.

Making the case—Part 2

Why how we talk to each other matters

It is through talking, that things get done, and that leadership and management are exercised. We can take for granted how we do our talking, until it doesn't work. Mostly it does, because we express ourselves in ways that are respectful, encouraging though sometimes challenging or decisive. We also know that sometimes it does not—the core theme of this book. We know this when we hear it. The aggressive, demanding, intolerant assertion of ideas and positions that leave others silenced. The talking that has a profound negative impact on the things we value and appreciate in ourselves, others and our teams.

What follows are notes to help consider the request to stop and pause to consider the substantive question, repeated here—*is the way we talk to each the best we can do to keep people safer and to work efficiently together and with others?*

Getting a conversation started

Imagine an informal conversation with a couple of people who have influence in the team or wider department. This is what you could talk about to engage people in an inquiry into talking.

Incivility and rudeness are inevitable in a busy team. Do we know what we mean by these behaviours?

A range of behaviours

- **Rudeness** is a lack of manners, discourteousness, impolite, insensitive or disrespectful behaviour by a person who has a lack of regard for others.

- **Incivility** is rudeness or unsociable behaviour / speech that occurs with ambiguous intentionality. It leaves the recipient wondering why and why me?

- **Bullying** is seeking to harm, intimidate, coerce, torment someone who is perceived as vulnerable.

Have we just gotten used to any of these behaviours? If we have, what other behaviours and attitudes have we come to accept, but would like to question because they 'hurt' in some way? For example:

What have we got used to?

Indifference
Casual rudeness
Swearing
Humiliation
Long hours
Exhaustion
Fear
Intrusion

...and not talking about the above

A reason to review our way of talking is these behaviours impact the things we value—our thinking and capacity, and our willingness to cooperate. That which makes us a good team/department to be in.

Effects to think about...

- Increased anger, fear and sadness and reduced optimism
- Feeling less committed to the organisation
- Lower levels of perceived fairness
- Decreased work commitment
- Engaging in retaliatory behaviours

See: Riskin, A., Erez, A., Foulk, T., Kugelman, A,. Gover, A. Shoris, I,. Riskin, K and Bamberger, P. (2015) The impact of rudeness on medical team performance: a randomised trial, Paediatrics, 136(3), pp.487-495.

We are paid to think. When we get together and, whether intentionally or not, we behave badly—our thinking is diminished. We become less able to bring our expertise to the work; we are less helpful; and are distracted. Basically, if I tell you to shut the ****up I am taking away what is most valuable from us and wider the organisation.

Impact on thinking

Adverse affect on the cognitive functions required for effective diagnostic and medical procedural performance.

May weaken the collaborative processes (information sharing and help-seeking) that can enable a team to compensate for any diminished performance in its membership.

See: Riskin, A., Erez, A., Foulk, T., Kugelman, A., Gover, A., Shoris, I., Riskin, K and Bamberger, P. (2015) The impact of rudeness on medical team performance: a randomised trial, Paediatrics, 136(3), pp.487-495.

You don't have to be the target of bad behaviour. Witnessing it is bad for us and the team.

Impact on bystanders...

- Decreased work commitment
- Decreased collaborative behaviours
- Emotional depletion
- Preoccupation with the 'event'

If we bully the effects are amplified.

How we can respond to incivility and bullying...

- We spend time trying to make sense of the situation.
- We reinterpret the event – they are just being clear; they are stressed; robust etc.
- Maybe this is normal for around here and I need to get used to it.
- Maybe it's my fault. Everyone else seems to get it. It is me who doesn't know what to do.
- I deserve this; I have been found out; I'm an imposter.

It can be useful to say you are not arguing that people will not and should never behave like the above. Effective teams do swear and shout and also, critically when things calm down, apologise and make reparation. Using the example of the more obvious silencing behaviours is a way into a broader conversation about all of the ways people get silenced and what would help them say more. That is more about what would improve the conversational culture. So that, more of the lived experience of the people, teams and departments could be spoken aloud and thought about, as data about how things work in practice. To move beyond any habitual downplaying of the challenges we face and to maintain the illusion that everything is fine. Otherwise, there is a risk it will be mentioned in the staff survey, then be subject to senior scrutiny and the possibility of simplistic interventions (be nicer; get HR more involved; get a consultant in).

Widening the conversation

Imagine the conversation has gone ok. There is an understanding of the impact of poor behaviour on the work.

However, there is less certainty about the presence and frequency of these behaviours in this team/department. You point out that maybe this small gathering is not a representative sample and perhaps others are sitting quietly also feeling unsafe. You agree to try and widen the conversation via a team meeting.

Let's assume your team or department is led by people who do not feel threatened by the process of stop and pause. Who understand that how people talk to each other is a factor in keeping people safer and running things effectively. They know that the cost of poor behaviour is hidden and high. They give the work their support and know that they will need to model the desirability to engage in this reflective practice. They will try and say more about their lived experience in the context of the ground rules you have briefed them on. You rough out a plan in your notebook to structure the hour.

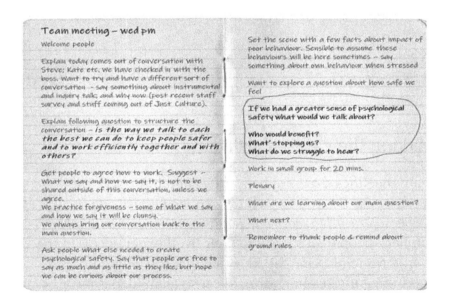

While no facilitation plan anticipates all that can happen when you introduce this topic, having a plan is useful. It offers a structure to guide and contain people. So that they feel they are in safe hands and, while they may be fed up you have already spoken to others and they were not included, you have done the groundwork with those who usually set the conversational tone. If this is the case then you have earnt the right to intervene if, and when, people behave in ways that make it less safe to do the work.

On a separate page, you might rehearse what you will do if people do behave unhelpfully.

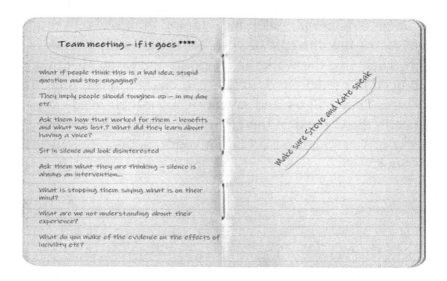

Making the case—Part 3

Team meetings structured and facilitated to explore the question—*is the way we talk to each the best we can do to keep people safer and to work efficiently together and with others?*— can help people give voice to their lived experiences. In the short-term reinforcing the idea that this sort of inquiry is a good thing to do. Short term, because team, department or organisational culture is rarely changed by a one-off event, lasting an hour. So, it is what happens next that is important to plan.

Keeping the conversation going

Conversational culture changes slowly, one conversation at a time. Key to keeping the question—can we do better?—front and centre, is to add an inquiry dimension to the conduct of everyday business. As we go about our work, we use it as an opportunity to think about how we do our talking. Specifically, how we construct and reinforce our assumptions, ideas and practices in relation to the following.

1. *What are we going to do?*
2. *How will we organise our resources to deliver our offer?*
3. *In whose interests are we acting?*
4. *Why this way of working rather than any other?*

If, in our daily conversations, we keep a critical eye on our answers and thinking to these questions, we can stay in touch with what we may be ignoring or silencing. How might this work in practice?

What to look out for

Is there too much agreement?

The absence of conflict is overrated. It can be a warning sign of a team locked into an unspoken agreement to privilege the wish of its members to belong and get along. Do this, rather than the harder work of thinking together about the four questions noted above.

Managers, team leaders, division directors can be judged (and can judge themselves), in terms of keeping order. For a few, keeping order means suppressing conflict and not listening to different voices and ideas. This may be necessary in an acute crisis, but it can become a habit. This does not mean that what is needed are loud, shouty meetings. Chronic disagreement ('who knows best what's best') can also be a distraction from the work of keeping in critical view the four questions. Work that needs people to collaborate on ideas and to question the current orthodoxy. This means a willingness to disagree, without collapsing into bullying and incivility, is a fundamental skill—if you want to keep people safer in complex environments.

A team that can hold the tension between agreeing and disagreeing has a capacity for 'argumentation'.[3] When such tension is held, people will feel encouraged to doubt, regardless of the rank or status of the speaker. The aim being to balance sense-making, to arrive at a valid account of the environment and the teams work in it, with sense-discrediting. That is, remaining sceptical and inquiring about who or what may be missing.

Questions to think about argumentation

- *What would it be like to question this person's account of how we need to organise?*
- *Who seems to be silenced?*
- *If they remain silent what perspective(s) on the work could be lost?*
- *Are we feeling a little too cosy, pleased with ourselves— why is that?*

Where are the conflicts?

Effective teams need to disagree and as noted above, this can become chronic, a form of avoidance. Conflict can be anchored in real differences and expressed in honest, kind ways. It can be the site of bad behaviour, driven by the wish to have one's own way and the fear of difference. Conflict, as argued in other chapters, suggests that buried in the interpersonal conflict are clues that point to something problematic in the way work is currently organised. Something that is hard to name and discuss so, best kept out of awareness, out of the team's day-to-day conversations. We should not kid ourselves that it is easy to lift collective heads out of a well-rehearsed interpersonal conflict. There is so much pleasure to be had in watching others fight and feeling like I am so much better than that. It is the work of the constructively awkward, to shift the focus. These questions can help provoke people's curiosity by asking aloud or by thinking about, as you participate.

■ *Who is disagreeing with who?*
■ *Why them, about this issue, in this meeting?*
■ *What might this conflict be pointing to in the work—something problematic we all need to think about?*
■ *What am I not understanding about this conflict/disagreement?*

What sort of silence is this?

This is a topic that might need a bit of explaining beforehand. We can tend to miss silence and when we do notice it, not attribute significant meaning to it. The following offers a language to name silences.

What sort of
silence is this...

- Aquiescent silence – people have given up, there is nothing to be done
- Defensive silence – people are just too scared to talk
- Pro-social silence – people are saying nothing to protect others or to protect an alliance or friendship
- Imposter silence – people are worried about sounding foolish
- Dominant silence – letting people know what it is ok to talk about - my silence is my approval

Silence can be assumed to be a personal choice, so pushing people to speak can feel wrong. The primary purpose of noticing silence is not to make people speak, or feel embarrassed, but to think about—*what sort of silence is this?* To see if it is possible to have a conversation to attribute meaning to the silence, which goes beyond the personal. Similarly, to exploring how interpersonal conflict can help surface things of relevance to the team, department or wider system. What can help, to get people talking about silence and its consequences, is talking about imposter syndrome.

Imposter syndrome

In any group of capable and ambitious people, some people (perhaps the majority) will be sitting in silence because of a chronic sense of inadequacy. This is despite evidence of their success. It is a sense of inadequacy built on feeling fraudulent and the attribution of any success to hard work, charm or luck. The feeling that one will be found out. It is a pervasive private feeling, shared by men and women, which can exacerbate any sense of 'I don't really belong here'. Not looking too clever; not saying anything that runs counter to the assumed norms around here. Silence seems like the sensible option. Understandable and one that can put at risk the task of keeping people safer.

If, in a group, half the people are struggling with feeling like imposters, it will have a profound impact on the conversations we can have. If you sit and observe you will notice the silences; the limited exploration of ideas; a lack of imagination; a wish to take the work outside of the group. You may notice the group is captured by a hubristic leader. He/she who has no time for self-doubt. You might hear complex situations flattened into problems that can be managed with current know-how, and the silencing of any questions about this.

What you are hearing and seeing is a consequence of treating imposter syndrome as just a personal characteristic, as if it were innate, inevitable.

Initiating an inquiry into silence and wider conversational culture is to talk about the external factors that can contribute to feeling like an imposter.[4] If I work in a culture that values confidence over competence; hates the anxiety of learning and rejects ignorance, I can be forgiven if I feel like an imposter. My self-doubt has no public expression, except in my head where it reinforces my sense of inadequacy. My doubts cannot be explored as possible clues about what we may all be struggling with. If we cannot talk about what we may be struggling with or avoiding, our project to keep people safer is put at risk.

Suggesting that a reason for silence is that some people are feeling like imposters and to argue that any form of silence, however personally felt, needs to be investigated is to invoke the ethics of intrusion.[5]

Working beyond the personal

Leading an inquiry into how we talk around here, is to step to the side of one's usual role. It is to take up a leadership role. You are deliberately going to try and 'do different' because you know that if you just do the same, then nothing much will change. Asking the questions described in this chapter is to assume the role of an 'insider researcher'. 'Insider'—because you are a part of the system you want to investigate. You want to 'render the familiar strange'.[6] To make public what is usually kept private. To attempt this is to be deliberately intrusive. To probe and question; to move beyond everyday descriptions and interpretations of what is going on. To subject the culture to critical questioning and justify this intrusion because it can keep people safer.

Conclusion

This chapter began with a familiar question—what is being asked of me in this situation? What can I do, when I am not the most senior person in the room, to seek agreement to stop and pause to question how we talk around here. Question how our conversational culture helps us focus on some ways of thinking and acting and silences others. The things we do not want to talk about; like; or know how to do.

A set of ideas has been described that can help gather support, to structure a conversation with colleagues and sustain this conversation over time. A process to nudge the culture along so that people are safer to say a bit more about what they experience, worry about and know. To enact such a process is without doubt an act of leadership. Not the leadership anchored in structural power and always knowing what to do but what Schein calls 'Humble Leadership'.[7] A leadership characterised by facilitation skills and helping people say more. Not only because people will work better together and bring more of their cognitive power and know-how to the work; but because it's the right thing to do. This is leadership anchored in the ethic of doing what it takes to keep people safer. It is not easy. It is the right thing to do.

Notes

1 Argyris, A. (2000) *Flawed advice and the management trap.* Oxford: Oxford University Press.
Argyris, C. (1991) Teaching smart people to learn. *Harvard Business Review*, 69(3), May–June, pp. 99–109.

2 Schein, E. (2013) *Humble inquiry. The gentle art of asking questions instead of telling.* San Francisco: Berrett-Koehler (see p. 100).

3 People dealing with dynamically complex environment:
'. . . *need to be able to develop intelligent ideas about the*

environment (sense making) but at the same time need to be able to criticise their ideas (sense-discrediting)' (p. 74).
Krammer, E.-H. (2007) *Organizing doubt. Grounded theory, army units and dealing with dynamic complexity.* Slovenia: Liber & Copenhagen Business School Press.
4   Olah, N. (2019) Imposter syndrome? It's a matter of class, not health. *The Guardian*, 17th October (Opinion section), p. 4.
5   Elam, G. and Fenton, K. (2003) Researching sensitive issues and ethnicity: Lessons learnt form sexual health. *Ethnicity and Health*, 8(1), pp. 15–27.
6   Goodley, D., Lawthom, R., Clough, P. and Moore, M. (2004) *Researching life stories.* London: Routledge Falmer.
7   Schein, E. (2018) *Humble leadership. The power of relationships, openness, and trust.* San Francisco: Berrett-Koehler.

Chapter 8

Walking off the map[1]

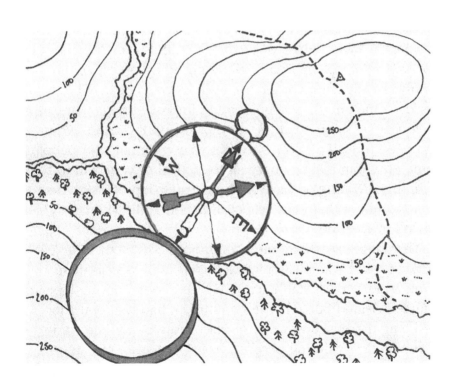

Most people will be quite confident of their naviga-
tion skills on a warm, clear, summer's day or while
following a well-marked footpath. The problem is that
these scenarios often do not last long: the weather can
change in an alarmingly brief time, signs run out,
tracks disappear or are impassable.[2]

Introduction

Previous chapters described moments when people were
silenced and explored the small changes people could try in a
meeting or conversation that could make things safer. To help
everyone get the job done now. This chapter explores the role
of senior leaders. When you realise that these small incidents
add up to a problem. That you are presiding over a culture
capable of silencing voices you really need to hear. When you
decide something has to be done to improve things that can
no longer be dumped at the door of your HR people. When
you need to lead a process to involve a wide range of people,
some of whom maybe angry and sceptical of your will to see
it through. When you have to show leadership of a process to
change culture that your acts of omission and commission had
a hand in creating.

The suggestions here emerged from a consultancy project
I undertook. I was invited into a department to help them
think about a poor staff survey. Where people reported feeling
intimidated and bullied. The department had the reputation
for being the best and worst of places to work. It had some
of the hardest working people I have ever met. Long hours
(70 plus was not unusual) and complex problems to solve. If
you can work here, you can pretty much do anything.

I worked with the senior team for four months. I failed to
help the senior team recognise and manage two contradictory thoughts. They knew that bullying and incivility could be

the day-to-day experience for their people. They knew this because they too were subject to such behaviour and could themselves express such behaviours. They also behaved as if these behaviours did not affect how they and others felt and thought. It is hard to lead a programme of work to improve things when such competing thoughts and assumptions remain unexamined.

This chapter is organised into two sections. Section 1 sets out seven things to think about and avoid as you consider commissioning and leading a project to address silencing behaviours. Section 2 imagines an alternative outcome of the consultancy project I undertook. This section offers a step-by-step guide as you intervene.

Section 1—What to avoid

Setting the scene

I am nervous. Sitting outside a meeting room, waiting to meet the director. I have been invited in to help because of my work to understand the effects of bullying and incivility. The senior team is on the back foot after a poor staff survey. Things need to improve quickly.

This is not my usual environment, but the complexity of their work is familiar. Doing a good job; working hard; not failing or complaining, matters around here. This team is multi-cultural, highly educated and motivated to make a difference in the lives of citizens.

Some of my anxiety is because I'm not sure what to do. Do I knock or just wait? I can see three people in the room. One of them is Cat, who has introduced me to her boss. I think I am being kept waiting. Eventually, I'm invited in. There is no preamble. I am asked by Anne, the department head, to explain my approach. The meeting reminds me of my viva.

Collegiate and competitive. Who knows best what's best. It lasts 20 minutes and ends abruptly. A quick thank you and I leave.

Cat calls me later. 'You passed'.

Seven mistakes

1. Not asking some questions as the work began

Looking back, I realise that as I sat outside the room, I was feeling pleased about being invited to help. I was also anxious about meeting Anne, a bit in awe of their place of work, what they did and who they were. As a result, I was not sufficiently curious as our first conversation unfolded. I told myself the real work would start later. So, what follows is hindsight.

The key lesson is the work starts at first contact. Holding three questions in mind can help everyone stay focused, in role, at an anxious moment.

- *What is preventing this team from leading the work themselves?*
- *Why are they deciding to act now?*
- *What do they want from their external help?*

These questions remain relevant as the work progresses. More information may reveal itself. Calling in the consultants is a standard response to a relationship crisis. Asking for help makes sense. It is a decision that needs to be recognised as a clue as well as an invitation to help. A clue about how the senior team is thinking about its authority to tackle what will obviously be difficult. A clue about the will to see it through. I failed to ask these questions and so silenced the senior team's ambivalence.

Astute people like them didn't need to read the research to know they were heading towards dangerous ground. They wanted to hear from their people, understand their experience and make it better. They cared about their people. They also knew but had not discussed with each other, that their authority to lead this work was contingent. Dependent upon their willingness to acknowledge that they were part of the problem. That they could behave in ways that were felt to be so problematic around here.

Leadership in this context required them to hold the tension between their responsibility for making it better and their sense of culpability. Holding this tension is a big ask of a leadership team that still has to run operations in a demanding environment. It was made harder because it was acknowledged early as the defining tension of the work. A tension that could disrupt their senior team and their relationships with their boss, Anne.

By failing to ask questions at the moment of beginning, this tension was left hidden. A no-go area. Confined to the private deliberation of individuals. How to manage this tension, an inevitable consequence of this work, was framed as a private struggle. Rather than what it actually was—a shared leadership task. Their 'framing' of the situation as personal meant they struggled to talk together. They were unable to explore how they would demonstrate a collective approach to acknowledging culpability and driving change to improve things.

It was this absent conversation that was the enduring consequence of my failure to recognise when the work began and to ask the three questions. Taking time at the beginning to scope the landscape and the implication for the leadership team is hard and can help manage the tensions more safely.

2. No one is free of sin

As we planned the approach, I assumed the senior team did not use or were not targets of the bullying behaviours described in the staff survey. I was wrong. As a consequence, I failed to help the senior team talk about their lived experience. This made it harder for them to listen to what other people said when invited to talk about their experiences. Some of the senior people were victims, carrying considerable distress. This made it hard for them to think about other people.

3. Failing to understand the culture of privacy

The work demands were huge, executed in a highly regulated environment. Everyone was under scrutiny. When I interviewed people, I found they were wary of saying anything that could be interpreted as weakness or incompetence. They held themselves to a high standard of self-control. Day to day they kept private how it felt being bullied and subject to everyday incivility. A form of self-silencing.

When invited to talk with me as part of the project, people welcomed it. They found talking, in the privacy of an interview to be cathartic and reassuring. However, for me and the leadership team to understand and make sense of what was going on across and/within the teams, these private conversations had to become 'public'. While what was reported was intensely personal, it was also data about what shaped their collective experience. What I failed to resolve was—how to go public with sufficient psychological safety.[3]

4. Do not disappoint people

I was able to get people to talk, but this was not enough. If you say to people, who have been harassed and bullied, that you want to listen—do not be surprised if they say clearly how ****ed-off they are.

I discovered that if the senior team is unprepared for how people can express themselves, two things can happen. The people invited to say how they feel are dismissed as too angry, too emotional. This allows the senior team to dump their ideas and insights. As if the best explanation for such overt emotion lies in the psychology of the individual. Maybe they lack the grit and determination required to work around here. Secondly, people's expectations for change will be disappointed, replicating and reinforcing a culture that silences discomforting data.

5. Not preparing the senior team

Little of what people said was heard without comment by the senior team who felt challenged. They felt challenged to manage contradictory demands. To improve things, to keep things stable, and to avoid being pressurised by their executive managers.

I did not make sure these demands were surfaced. As such, the senior team could not talk about how things were and how impossible that felt at times. This translated into a reluctance to hear what people complained about. They found ways to counter peoples' lived experience.[4] This exposed the senior team to the charge of not listening or caring; of being incapable of improving things.

6. Don't paint the boss into a corner

I did not notice something obvious. Anne's role as director made her different in the senior team. As a consequence, I missed the enormous pressure Anne was under. She was shouldering a complex leadership task. She wanted to improve the department's culture and do this in an organisation led by an executive that could replicate the very behaviours that were so problematic. Anne had to ensure it was safe enough for anyone, who wanted, to speak. She had to help her senior people manage the consequences of any feedback; she had to satisfy her executive. Finally, Anne had to demonstrate the value of lowering one's defences and allowing one's behaviour to be scrutinised, to drive the work forward.

Failing to make this complex set of tasks explicit and providing a safe space for her to think, forced Anne onto the defensive; as it would anyone.

7. Not engaging with the executive

The power of the executive to affirm or authorise the questioning of the existing culture was obvious. People talked about meetings in which the most senior people behaved badly. The plan we developed for the department was ok. I now know I shut my eyes to the question of how to engage the executive. It was too difficult. As a consequence, I helped paint Anne into a corner.

Recognising this omission does not mean I now know what to do. A recent invitation to do similar work did not progress because the senior leadership recognised the risks of what I was proposing and they had no reason to trust me. Part of the difficulty is that executives can behave as if the problem of bad behaviours lies elsewhere in the organisation. So, any move to engage them threatens this defence. What it does suggest is the importance of keeping the role of the most senior people in mind and being ready to see it as a pressure that falls to the leaders of any intervention. Pressure that may show up as a reluctance to move things forward.

Conclusion

Trying to improve things, make it safer to speak, is the right thing to do. It's a duty of leadership. It's also the case that it's a process that has to be informed by a realistic description of the terrain to come. It's not a simple sunny walk in the park with a well-laid-out footpath and a café halfway around. Most critical is understanding that if you ask people to speak up, they will. They will say things that will tempt you to shut them up again.

The next section offers a step-by-step approach that reduces the risk of making the sort of mistakes I made. A final point. The interviews left me in no doubt of the cost that people (and their families and clients) pay for a leadership that fails to see how it can silence people and that fails to try and improve things.

Section 2—a step-by-step guide

Introduction

The steps described here are by necessity destabilising. The silencing of others can be an ingrained habit of leadership.[5] People know they should be nicer, and they know this advice is insufficient to change behaviour or help others to do so. These behaviours are resilient. The steps described here are designed to dislodge familiar ways of thinking and behaving.

If one imagines a department or organisation as an urban landscape, with familiar roads and routes, then leading an intervention to improve things needs the heart of an urban explorer. Someone who can walk the familiar streets and be curious, seeking the hidden places.[6] The places where the difficult questions lurk. The places that have big fences and security. The places that represent the no-go areas in a team or department. The places where people can feel affronted at being questioned. They may experience it as a form of trespass onto their preferred way of making sense of the world; a trespass that feels like a challenge to their authority. And, as you roam the streets never forget you are part of that landscape and have helped to shape it.

Like previous chapters, I have imagined a different outcome to the work I was involved in. Again, describing modest interventions that can improve things, that are doable alongside delivering the day job. The steps will not be a perfect fit for your organisation or department but hopefully they are presented in sufficient detail to be the basis for a planning conversation.

Six steps

1. Prepare the senior person

The meeting went as it did and I still passed. I make my involvement contingent on a follow-up meeting with Anne. It's my turn to talk and see if we can work together. We meet on a Tuesday in a quiet office, and I ask:

> *Before I accept the invitation, can we talk about how this sort of work can play out? This conversation is important because you are the sponsor of this work. Your role is already hard enough and this work will add to the load. I need to brief you on what can happen as you try and improve things.*
>
> *There is no easy way to say this, but what you want to do will put you and your senior team at risk. In our first meeting, you said you wanted people to feel safer to speak up and that maybe I can help with this. I can, but I need to say that when you make this offer and people speak, they will say things that will make you wish they would just be quiet again. I think it's fine to think this. It means you're listening. Not everything said will be valid or require a response. But some of it will point to how things are for some people. The braver people will name names, including maybe you and your team. It's horrible to hear and is*

the first big moment of the work—holding your nerve and helping your colleagues to do so. If you dive in and shut things down, it's best not to begin.

This sort of intervention is problematic because what may be said will fall under your HR policies. You need to frame the intervention in a way that foregrounds your desire to understand what is driving us to behave badly, while not standing in the way of an individual's right to access relevant policies.

There are a couple of other things I have to draw your attention to, then I'll shut up.

I know you want to increase people's sense of psychological safety—I think that's right, but you need to include yourself in that. In your role you are already exposed, so to lead this project you will need a place and person(s) to keep you honest, a place where you can express how hard this is, so you can keep thinking even when the next step is unclear.

My last point is you need to make it safe enough for your senior team. I think this means you need to take a step back and kindly ask them to think with you. To resist blaming people for taking up the invitation to speak; and perhaps the most difficult, sponsor a conversation about how these behaviours may be present in your team.

A senior person has the position and authority to enable this project and to condemn it to failure. Failure is the outcome when someone like Anne does not have a safe enough place to talk about the challenges of leading this intervention.

Imagining that this conversation has gone well, Anne realises a couple of things. She must step back from her senior team, to hold them to the task of making things safer. Not in a demanding, measuring, surveillance way but in an enabling way: *If I ask you to do this what do you need from me and each other?*

This question leads to the second step.

2. Preparation of the senior team

There are six people in the room. Anne has asked me to brief her senior team on the plan and the risks. Anne begins by summarising our recent conversation; the uncertainty she now feels; and that no decision to proceed can be made until she knows if her senior team is up for it. She invites me to speak.

> *Anne has asked me to be blunt so there is less doubt about the work ahead. There are two things we need to cover in the next two hours. The first is an out-line of the stages of a constructive intervention. The second is the stuff you need to think about together before you go live.*
>
> *The intervention has six stages. The first two are about what you are doing now. The senior people having this time to think in private. The third is when the work goes 'public' because you invite people to individual interviews. A conversation where you are asking people to talk about their experience of work. You know this carries risks and I will come back to this in a minute.*
>
> *The fourth stage is developing with people, valid and practical ideas about what is driving the poor behaviours reported in the staff survey and the stage three interviews. Stage five is agreeing on small actions to test what improves things, and the final stage is about integrating these changes into everyday ways of thinking and behaving.*
>
> *You will be anticipating some of the challenges but let me set out what I think you need to talk about.*

If you invite people to speak, they will say positive stuff but some of it will be hard to hear. People will try to be balanced in what they say. They understand there are pressures and that we can all behave badly sometimes. But you have to be prepared for the tough stuff. The details of being bullied and being treated badly. Names, places, the forensic details. It's entirely normal for you to want to shut them up again.

Anne speaks.

What's hard is we cannot pretend that we have not expressed some of these behaviours, been on the receiving end or stood by. No surprise, but I have not always been kind. I'm sorry and I am tempted to run a million miles away from this work. Stick up a few posters about being kind and dump it in HR. Sorry, Chris.

The temptation of 'business as usual'

The meeting continues.

People agree that they face an ethical moment. They can choose to do nothing. Disguising this decision by saying encouraging things about 'compassion' and being nice.

The risk is people will see them for what they believe and want. For people to keep private aspects of their experience of work. That bad behaviour and the attrition rate of good and clever people is an acceptable trade for business as usual—the real win here.

If the senior team asks people to speak up, the data has to be followed up and interpreted. Even if this means they are uncertain how to do this or where it will end up. The upside is that others may believe their intention to face facts and to try and right a wrong.

Back to the group

Chris, director of HR suggests.

> *We have tried dealing on a case-by-case basis. We have tried to help line managers take a more inquiry-based approach and use formal procedures as a last resort. None of the people we work with are stupid. The informal systems are full of stories of bad behaviour. What if we assumed most people know that in this environment the causes are complex? People want to work here but wonder why it's so hard, why it's so inefficient.*
>
> *What if we began our work in public by acknowledging the research on bullying and incivility—that we foreground the importance of people being able to bring their best thinking to the work? We don't present this as primarily the resolution of individual stories—though I will insist if people want to use the procedures they can, and I will support them.*
>
> *We present this as a shared effort—to investigate and understand how these behaviours are triggered; the roles we can take up; and what we can do to reduce the risks and make it a bit safer.*

Chris's intervention tips the balance toward investigation. Aja thanks Chris and says he wants to add something.

> *The invite to speak up is right, but it will be heard differently. We cannot assume this is a simple invitation. Some will be suspicious, particularly those who have felt marginalised or unwelcome. We need to monitor who we are reaching. I think the other thing is—we are going to have to talk about our behaviour. That will be fun.*

Anne suggests a way forward.

> *Can we agree on some ground rules if we are going to do this? First up, what is said here stays here. If we are going to feel safe to talk, we cannot name names outside—it's the themes we are after. Second, let's not just focus on people who have been bullied or perpetrators. I have witnessed some bad behaviour and not said anything. Finally, let's just keep talking.*

The senior team agrees on the approach, tacitly acknowledging they cannot behave as if all the issues are out in the staff group. They can behave badly towards each other. They begin an awkward conversation about this fact while leading the next step of the work.

They agree on the text of a letter to people setting out their aims for the work. It's signed by Anne and Chris. Anne signs it to show she is leading this work and will hold her team to account. Chris signs it to remind people of the rule of law. People are not being asked to surrender their right to access the HR procedures.

The email—asking for help

> *In response to the staff survey and recent events, we want to develop a different approach to what we have called unprofessional behaviours. We need to uncover and then tackle the underlying issues that are adversely affecting people's ability to do their work. The research we have read is clear. Being on the receiving end of bullying and incivility affect how we think; how we feel and how we can collaborate to get things done. Saying we want things to change is not the same as knowing how to do it.*

What we do know is that we need to find a way to ask people to talk about their lived and felt experience of work here. In asking this we are asking you to trust that we are in listening mode and that we know we also have to think hard about our involvement in what is going on.

We want to invite you to a semi-structured interview with X. We have asked her to help because while we need to lead this process, we also must not get in the way of people speaking. We have asked X to provide a confidential and safe enough space for you to talk about how you feel and experience your work. When it goes well and when it doesn't.

X will collate themes that will support us to have a conversation about what we think are the drivers for our unprofessional behaviours and what can help us step back from silencing others; being silenced; being bystanders to behaviours that undermine our capacity to work together to keep people safer.

This invitation is tricky. You are free to say as much or as little as you like. If it becomes clear that people are currently subject to bullying behaviours, X will ask you what you would like to do. To be on the receiving end of bullying and incivility is harmful to individuals and those who are witness to it. It can also be a clue about what is hard to talk about around here. If we could find a way of talking about these issues, we will be less likely to use these unprofessional behaviours.

While we want to understand what organisational business is being transacted via these intensely personal behaviours, we also want people to feel safe. If we need to intervene and you agree, we will do so using existing HR procedures.

To summarise, the plan is to convene a series of confidential conversations, the content of which will be synthesised into themes. We will then agree on a process to think through what we now know about what drives our unprofessional behaviours and what may help reduce its frequency. As a first step have a look at the summary of the research on the effects of bullying and incivility.

To contact X . . .

Assume the letter lands well. People like the humility of the senior people and the interviews begin.

3. Talking

People speak freely. The senior team battles with its desire to shut it all down and holds its nerve. It's a 'Pandora's box' moment and hope is yet to emerge. Some people are very cross and very upset. The interviews are characterised by the following.

*We want to work here, we can do good things and feel like we are making a difference, but why is it so ****ing hard? I do not want to feel this exhausted, be ignored, humiliated in a meeting, or receive texts at 3 am and feel I have to respond.*

Loads of data are gathered and several themes are identified, and a draft report is produced. The senior team again notice their desire to manage how the report lands; to anticipate what actions will be required. Again, Anne asks the team to wait and see what people have to say.

4. Sensemaking

A series of meetings is held to discuss the draft report. Each meeting is led by Chris. The themes are felt to reflect the interviews, but people feel they have been toned down—shorn of feeling. People are angry with the consultant working for Anne. They express this towards the senior team and the consultant.

There are moments when Chris notices he wants to respond and protect his colleagues. He mostly holds his silence. People get he is trying hard. They are struck by a comment he makes.

> *We are in a tricky place. You need to know its ok if you want to pursue the HR route. Some of what has gone on is unacceptable. It's been on my watch. I also know that if we are going to make progress, we have to dig into why we behave like this. Otherwise, I have to accept that people are stuck in a role and that I have managed to recruit a bunch of high performing psychopaths.*
>
> *I don't believe that. I have to assume people can get out of roles, otherwise we are all stuck. Stuck as bystanders, bullies, and victims.*
>
> *We need to try and understand why we use these behaviours and why they can go unchallenged. We need to think together about what people have said. Then to build that understanding and acknowledge that people have not had it easy. For that, I apologise.*

People agree to make their own decision about accessing the HR route. They agree to work in small groups to 'work below the surface' of their accounts and develop a tentative theory about what drives these poor behaviours/roles and what should be done to mitigate them.

One group explores in detail those moments when people lose it and start shouting. They focus less on what is said and more on the consequences of the shouting and swearing. That is, who and what gets silenced; and how this leads to the absence or hiding of data. Data that may be useful in managing the substantive issues people face in their day-to-day work.

Another group reads the literature on by-standing. They note it's a hard role to give up and a crucial one if silence is no longer to be read as tacit agreement. Agreement and therefore support to whoever is shouting and swearing.

5. Small actions

The work of the groups and informal conversation marks a change in the attitude of most of the staff group team. The prevailing assumptions—*'people should toughen up'; 'I was just being robust and clear'*—have been outed as inadequate self-serving explanations.

A more sophisticated view about behaviour and roles is emerging. In one of the groups Sarah, a team leader offers an observation.

> *I hate to say this, but this way of behaving is not going to just go away. The pressure and deadlines will never get any less. Telling people to be nice never works, can we do something to disrupt things as they happen? Not wait till afterwards when the damage has already been done?*
>
> *The more I think about it, sitting in silence when someone is being told to 'shut the **** up' makes it worse. Maybe this is what turning a blind eye and deaf ear is about, a sort of encouragement to others to carry on regardless and leave others feeling like they are on their own.*

A small shift is being negotiated about how the roles of bully, victim and bystander are understood. Anyone can be trapped in one of the roles and knowing that does not let people off the hook of thinking and behaving differently to make things safer.

They ask Chris to take a rough plan to Anne and the senior team. The plan has four components.

1. Agree a means to authorise anyone to call 'stop' when bad behaviours erupt. In the pause, ask people to think about why things have taken a turn for the worse. What is it about the issue being discussed that is so problematic that these behaviours are required?
2. Agree how to authorise anyone to back up or second this call for a pause by saying something like 'I think this as well—we need to stop, pause and think'.
3. Add questions to an interim staff survey to gather examples of how the stop and think intervention is working in practice.
4. Ask the senior team to model 'stop and think' and back it up when the request is resisted—we have agreed to do this. We need to stop as asked.

Chris has a productive conversation with Anne, who adds another point.

> *Chris, this job is not suddenly going to be easier.*
> *I agree with what is being said and I know I will be*
> *one of those who slip up. You know how I can be.*
> *I will say the odd JFD comment. I need to work in a*
> *place where that odd slip can be tolerated. So, I want*
> *a group set up to think about this inevitability and*
> *what reparation is required. Senior leaders can be*
> *shit at saying sorry.*

6. The everyday

People in the day-to-day meeting of the department experiment with 'stop, pause, think' as they work. They notice they talk about this as if they know how to do it. They do not.

A small team is set up to run a series of simulations to explore what helps. They talk about what people have noticed when they have spoken up. It's a sorry list.

- The only voice in the room left swinging.
- You are carrying everyone's responsibility to think about how business is conducted within agreed policies.
- People looking away at their devices.
- Taking silence as evidence of your misjudgement and support to whoever you are trying to question.
- Being bollocked outside of the meeting by your line manager for showing them up.
- Getting support after the meeting.

In the simulation, they experiment with a seconder role. This role is a way to embed the shared responsibility for checking bad behaviour.

They decide to experiment by putting people into virtual/ad hoc quads in meetings. After the draft trial and error, people come up with two rules.

Rule one. If someone in your quad asks a meeting to stop and think about how it's conducting its business, all three back them up—we need to stop—no question.

Rule two. To back someone up is not to be taken as agreement with what they go on to say. The intervention of the three is to publicly protect and reinforce the right of any citizen in this organisation to call a group, of whatever seniority and task, to stop, pause and think—even for a few minutes.

The group meets with the senior team and ask that this approach is authorised by them. That as senior leaders, they say to people this approach is binding on everyone in the department.

Within the department, this approach gains traction. There was a moment when a new senior person ignored the request. A senior colleague took him to one side and explained this was not how they did things here. The newcomer said sorry and that he had not been properly briefed.

This incident resulted in work, led by Chris and Anne, to change the way new people were recruited and inducted. Rather than dumping a policy file in people's laps and giving PowerPoint presentations, they introduced a conversation section. They titled it: *what we were like and why we don't do that anymore*. The aim, to pass on the history, brief new people into the research on behaviours, including by standing; and what is now expected of people.

Closing comments

This is a chapter for people in leadership roles, who accept their responsibility for shaping the conversational culture of their team; department; or organisation. People who are also part of the systems they want to question and make safer for talking. People who know their own behaviour, replicates and reinforces what enables and what silences. People who may be subject to the very behaviours they know need to change.

I hope I have made the case that intervening on a poor conversational culture is the right thing to do and a hard thing to do. Encouraging people to find their voice and speak about their lived experience, good and bad, is usually rewarded with a crisis. When people speak up, some of what they have to say will trigger a wish to shut them up again. People will be passing comment on the sort of place the leadership have created, by their behaviour and systems of work. Some of what is said will be hard to hear and to tolerate. Leadership at this moment is about how this crisis is faced. I have suggested that talking before going 'public,' is useful in terms of developing the sort of emotional, relational and cognitive agility that is required to not shut people down again.

I have listened to a senior team grappling with this crisis. Talking about how they have shut people down; imposed an acceptable organisational view of things. Not just out there in their organisation but here in this room. It was a messy conversation and it was emotional but it felt real. These were seriously capable people who accepted the responsibility for the conversational culture that shaped all aspects of their organisation. From performance reviews to informal conversations in the café. They talked about how they were with each other as a team and how this helped set the tone. They wanted to lead an organisation where feeling and ideas could be expressed freely, bounded by the shared task—the well-being of the citizens and communities they served. A challenging task and the right one to justify their attention to how people did their talking as they went about their work.

Notes

1 Macfarlane, R. (2008) *Mountains of the mind*. London: Grant.
2 Brotherton, L. (2011) *The ultimate navigation manual*. London: Collins, p. 12.
3 Edmonson, A. (2019) *The fearless organisation. Creating psychological safety in the workplace for learning, innovation, and growth*. Hoboken, NJ: Wiley.
4 Counter resistance—seeking to counter innovation, change or new data. Tactics may include argument, concept rejection or demand for quick and comprehensive spread, delays in

responding, silencing other staff and presence or absence from meetings.

Caygill, H. (2013) *On resistance. A philosophy of defiance.* London: Bloomsbury.

5　For an explanation of this sort of leadership, see Kellerman, B. (2004) *Bad leadership. What it's, how it happens, why it matters.* Boston: Harvard Business School Press.

6　Find the: ' . . . *alternative landscapes and hidden places behind doors, through fences and under manhole covers we pass every day*' (p. 242).

Garrett, B. (2013) *Explore everything. Place hacking the city.* London: Verso.

Chapter 9

Staying hopeful

DOI: 10.4324/9781003302322-9

*'. . . I am left making a value judgement about
whether or not to speak up in the face of too little
information or confidence to make that very decision.
I guess what I mean is that if I had enough info. and
experience (in relation to those I'm with) I would not
be having the conversation with myself about whether
or not to speak up! . . . I find it really frustrating and
total illogical nonsense'.*[1]

Introduction

In this concluding chapter, I want to investigate what is possible at the moment when it feels too scary to speak. When
you want to speak, find you cannot and do not want to lose
your grip on that all-important question—*what is being asked
of me in this situation?* When you want to keep thinking about
what is going on and why; and what you would like to say if
things felt safer.

This chapter describes what you can try, to keep thinking
and avoid collapsing into an acquiescent self-blaming silence.
A state of affairs that leaves a conversation thin and superficial.
Of course, not everyone feels like this. They seem to speak up
with ease. Here are two examples.

Testing the leadership

It is the second day of a five-week leadership programme for
community leaders. There are 25 of them and three of us, the
programme directors. I had been outlining the programme
structure, emphasising that we would be working 'below the
surface' to explore the factors that influence our behaviour and
sense of authority as leaders. One of the participants raises a
hand and asks the following.

'Do you know what it is like for some of us to be faced by three white programme directors?'

His intervention defines a dimension of constructive awkwardness. It was a blunt, clearly delivered, surprising, authority-challenging, assumption-probing intervention. He sought to question our understanding of what we might represent as white directors to black participants. In particular, to test our capacity to participate in conversations that explored how we might collectively re-create those aspects of structures that some found oppressive. That is, as we asked them to critically reflect upon their behaviour, could we, would we, do the same? Or were we going to use our role as directors to not do the work with them. His intervention created a pause, a moment.

The critical thing about his intervention was that it did not stop the three of us thinking. The intervention was pitched in a way that facilitated, albeit uncomfortably, a collaborative enquiry, where agreement was not the purpose but an exploration of different ideas.

On the Oxford train

My colleague told me this story. He was on the early train from Oxford to London. He related how he had stood up in a crowded train and addressed the carriage about the effects of the many mobile phone users on the experience of those wishing to sit and think. A reporter captured the event.

The terribly polite, middle-class war against mobile phones on trains strikes its first blow. Just as we were coming into Paddington on Thursday morning, a man just behind me in the carriage, a man

*in late middle age wearing a grey suit, made a
rather brave and noble speech. 'I'm going to say this
very loudly,' he said, very loudly. 'I find it extremely
annoying when somebody conducts a long and
loud business conversation on their mobile phone
while sitting opposite me on a train. It does not have
to be so loud, nor continue for so long. And for those
of us who are trying to read or analyse documents
or just look out of the window and think, I find it
absolutely paralyses the thought processes. If anyone
agrees with me, perhaps you would be kind enough
to make a supportive noise.' As for the man responsible for Thursday's offending mobile-phone conversation, he said softly to the complainant: 'There is a
quiet carriage further up the train where nobody is
allowed to use mobiles. You could always have sat
in there.' 'I most certainly would have done,' continued the complainant, just as loudly, 'except that
every seat was taken. Anyway, it is my view that
there should not be one carriage reserved for those
who do not like to listen to mobile phone conversations. There should be a carriage reserved for those
who wish to make them, and you can all bellow
together'.*[2]

In my world, these are both audacious interventions. I can
only aspire to be so free to speak. Both were trained. One
a barrister and performance poet, the other a priest. Both
answered the question—*what is being asked of me?* by
speaking to what they felt might be hidden and useful to
surface. There was little hesitation and not much doubt in
their voices. In the leadership programme suggesting the
presence of racism but wrapped in the words of learning.
In the train, pointing to the unacknowledged blurring of the

boundary between the right to do business and to be quiet. The one time I called someone out for playing their music loud I got the wrong person. Many of us will have had the same thoughts and insights and sat in silence. We can look to the heroes, the easy speakers. We should certainly respect their skills but trying to be like them may be less useful than exploring the ordinary, everyday experience of having things to say but staying quiet.

The way of the ordinary

We know that staying quiet makes everyone a bit less safe. We know that we should help create a culture of openness, where we feel obliged to be candid. Each time there is a formal inquiry into things going wrong, the resulting report has a familiar set of recommendations. For example:

- A culture of openness, transparency and candour; where we have a duty of candour (Francis report, 2013).[3]
- A culture that supports and encourages people to make complaints and raise concerns (NHS investigations into matters relating to Jimmy Saville, 2015).[4]
- A commitment to a culture of openness and honesty (Learning from Bristol, 2001).[5]

I believe that the reason for these repetitions is the assumption that we are all capable of being that person on the train or the one calling out the directors. I think a safer assumption is that we are not like this in any reliable way. This means we need to find a way of making our silence into a tool of resistance. We may be quiet, but we are still thinking, doing our job, capable of speaking if things change a bit. What follows is an exploration of what it may take to make a silence, that is in danger of slipping into acquiescence and being misread as my agreement, into an active silence.

What is an active silence?

It is the capacity to keep thinking when it feels dangerous to speak and being ready to seek out connections with others, when the time feels right. Maybe I have been told to shut the **** up; or have heard that said to others. Where the leadership of the meeting is so pacey it feels really hard to interrupt the flow. That I will really stand out and as such, I had better be right if I do speak. It is to experience all this and keep thinking about what is going on and thinking about how one is going to answer that basic question—*what is being asked of me right now in this situation?* Sometimes, the right response is—*I need to stay safe, keep thinking and reach out to others when I can.*

Active silence is anchored in Zeldin's way of the weak, first described in Chapter 1. This is the use of quiet interventions to dislodge a more powerful person's attachment to their thinking, without arousing their counter-resistance. That is, their wish to push away ideas, opinions, or people that do not confirm their view of things. As such, active silence is a part of the tactical tool kit of the constructively awkward. It is also in the tool kit of people who meet political violence with non-violence.[6] People who argue that nonviolence is not weakness or acquiescence but an act of resistance. Specifically, the refusal to give up hope in relation to our interconnectedness with others. The connections that bullying, incivility and tyranny seek to break. Not always consciously, of course, but this tends to be the result. That is why, after a difficult meeting, I will seek out people to say what I would have said in support of them. To say what felt impossible at the time, to confirm our social ties. So, the question is, what might help us to remain hopeful that the time will come when we can speak freely?

How do I remain hopeful?

If remaining hopeful is an act of resistance, it is an act grounded in a capacity to think. If thinking is what we must try and do, so as not to have our cognition overwhelmed by feeling, what we think about is key. Key to sustaining this capability and using it to stay hopeful. What follows are examples that can sustain one's hope. Help one stay in the room; stay connected; and think about taking a small step to disrupt things. Hope that is based on facing a fundamental dilemma and then asking some questions of ourselves.

How do I manage the dilemma of belonging?

However confident I feel, joining a team is always a moment of anxiety. A few days ago I was on a Zoom call with a team I had been invited to join. The work was interesting, I thought I would be able to make a contribution. On the call I was careful how much I spoke and heard myself caveating what I was saying, in a jokey voice *'maybe I don't understand the work yet . . . but'*. My internal voice is shouting—you're nearly 65 you stupid ****, why are you still worrying about being liked, not overstepping the mark; showing off or any of those stupid childhood messages you have taken in about knowing your place. You're here to do a job, otherwise why in the **** did they ask you to join?

I had fallen into the most basic of dilemmas—belonging, collaborating and being myself. Forgetting that my public actions are grounded in how I manage this private tension. Do

I speak up; go against the flow of thinking in the team and risk (in my head at least) being marginalized and being asked to leave. Or do I moderate my words to minimise the risk of feeling the anxiety inherent in what Butler[7] describes as the 'vexations of social relationships' (p. 201)?

Assessing the risk of too much or too little voice, is not an entirely rational or conscious process. Past experiences, particularly bad ones, can significantly determine our choices. Ten years ago I was part of another team. We knew each other from other work. We liked and respected each other. We had got used to how each other spoke. The tone, volume, language and about what. We had become adept, without ever really discussing it, at ensuring we never strayed too far from agreement.

Friends fall out

Our task was to help four organisations, who had secured funding from our client, to innovate new ways of delivering services. The funding came with a requirement: to gather up what people were learning about 'doing' innovation in complex services. Our role was to facilitate this 'knowledge capture'. Work we approached as if we already knew how to do it and what to capture.

Assuming we knew enough, made it harder to hear the talk, circulating in the informal spaces of the projects. People were struggling to translate their carefully crafted plans into practical action. Why were innovative ideas not being taken up? Did project teams just need to try harder and write their guidelines more clearly? Did we need to coach people to be better project leaders?

We decided to try harder and help people with implementation, based on what we knew. Over the months as the projects continued to struggle, this approach began to feel limiting and part of the problem. However good we were, how carefully we executed our plans, it was not going to be enough.

A colleague and I said we wanted to talk about what we might be missing. That maybe we were stuck with what we knew and we were not looking hard enough into the many tactics of people who felt each project's pressure to change. That maybe we needed to learn about the many facets of resistance. That we were in danger of replicating the assumption in the project teams that resistance was the act of a few ill-informed individuals. People who had to be silenced or persuaded to face their ignorance. It felt a step too far to suggest that maybe we were in a parallel process. What was going on in the teams was alive and well in us. Could we step beyond our familiar knowledge to try something new?

The only attempt to talk about how our thinking might be limiting us, led us to polarising into two sub-groups. As if we had irreconcilable differences that were best managed by arguing. It was if we suddenly couldn't talk in an objective way. As if we could not think about why we were behaving like this at this moment in the life of the project.

The content of our various arguments are not the issue here. Each person, each subgroup could claim they knew interesting and useful stuff. The issue was we could not have a conversation that took us beyond our certainty. It was if something more important was at stake—the cohesion of the group. The perception of the group as a safe place that knows what it is doing.

I saw the warning signs in my own anxiety. These were my friends. Trusted, able, thoughtful, kind colleagues. I wanted to shut up—but kept pushing. Then it was over. I found myself outside of the group. This was at least ten years ago. We have since made amends. I recount this story here because it is usually in my mind when I think about speaking out, going against the grain, saying something I suspect will be heard as criticism. This leads to another question. *How do I satisfy my need to belong, feel safe and do my job and speak to what I think I know?* I can remind myself of the following.

Think in terms of a dilemma

As we sit in a meeting thinking about saying something that feels a bit challenging to the prevailing ideas, we face this dilemma of belonging. Say it and be myself, express my individuality versus say it and risk losing my sense of place and comfort in this group, and feeling like I have let myself down in some way. This is a defining dilemma and a key feature of any dilemma is that it cannot be resolved.[8]

My colleague uses the example of breathing. She asks: *what is better—breathing in or out?* So, is it better to belong; collaborate and align myself to others to see what we can achieve? Or to remain separate and capable of questioning everything and risk being ejected from the group/team? To keep people safer we need both. This means the dilemma has to be 'held', managed or regulated, in such a way that both 'horns' of the dilemma are kept in view. Most interventions to get people to speak up, fail to acknowledge that this dilemma shapes how we take up the challenge of candour, in busy complex organisations, where teamwork is key. As if there is a wish to keep things simple. This is unhelpful.

Most people experience this dilemma of belonging; and think of it as a personal matter and a private challenge. Such an explanation may be correct and is an insufficient explanation. In the case studies in this book, the interpersonal dimension of this dilemma is apparent. Speaking up or staying quiet is strongly influenced by how others behave. If we confine this dilemma to the realm of the personal, we miss an opportunity for a public conversation. A conversation about belonging and how fragile this can feel. A conversation that strengthens our social connections and helps us feel a bit safer.

What if I listen to the conversation in my head?

What I say out loud is always an edited version of what
I know, see, sense, suspect is going on. It is the gap between
my lived experience as we go about our work and what I feel
safe enough to disclose. My evidence for this 'gap' is a recent
meeting. The meeting was to brief a group of experienced
leaders on a major policy development that would have significant implications for the way people thought about their sector
and their leadership.

Listed below (not in order) is what I thought and did not
say as the meeting played out.

- *What in the **** are you talking about?*
- *No idea what that acronym means, should I ask?*
- *I wish you would just slow down.*
- *Should I have said that?*
- *You have real courage to let people see how you feel about
  all the people who have died.*
- *Please shut up, enough information, what do you mean
  . . .?*
- *Are we being too hard on you, should I say something?*

Not all inner conversations are for sharing but neither should
they be summarily dismissed. It can be useful to think of
these internal monologs as potential lines of inquiry. A means
to explore what may be going on in our conversation, which
is yet to surface and may be useful to name. As such, my
focus of attention was also outwards to the meeting. This
helped me stay an active participant, even though I was silent.
I wasn't just 'stuck' in my head.

I was not alone in being troubled by not understanding
acronyms, feeling this was not a straightforward presentation
and wondering why I felt so emotional. I felt a bit more connected to others in the room who were also quiet. If I was not

on my own, then maybe if I spoke, others would come in and support me, or if someone else spoke I could add my support. Then a brave soul spoke directly to our speaker:

> *I understand you have a job to do and you're being clear with us but I'm sitting here feeling so angry. Once again, our sector has to align to you. I hear the words 'collaborate,' 'engage' but it sounds like it is on your terms. I'm sorry to be so blunt but we are here to talk.*

Her move, from silence to speaking, unlocked a conversation about power. Other people spoke to acknowledge how they were feeling; following her example of describing feelings and not expressing them directly. The conversation named the power asymmetry hidden in the language of 'engagement' and 'alignment'. How this unacknowledged asymmetry triggered a worry that there would be consequences if people sounded critical. How in the real world of services, this silence, based on a fear of retaliation would disrupt the direction of travel set out in this policy. A direction people agreed was correct.

To finish the story. The speaker was astute, capable and understood that when she walked into the room, she was the representative of the most powerful organisation in the room. Rather than this asymmetry not being acknowledged and a silencing influence on the conversation, it became available, with the speaker's assent, something we could talk about. We went from an individual, noisy, anxious silence to a conversation that could inform how real-world negotiations required by this policy, might be understood and facilitated.

Giving credibility to our internal conversation built our individual insight and inter-connectedness. It kept us working and built our sense of purpose, our sense of agency. It kept a variation of that basic question in mind—*what is being asked of me and us, right now?*

Do I want to talk about this issue right now?

To explore this question I want to use an experience of being a member of a support group that met once a week.

There are about 25 people in the room from across the service, sitting in a circle. Most of the different grades and professions are present. People are chatting with people next to them. The usual mess of coffee cups. There is an empty chair. At 3:00 pm the consultant leading the group walks in and sits down. There is immediate silence. Our task is to talk about our work, which by any standards is difficult, emotional and sometimes scary. I look around and see the people I work with every day. I see my manager and his manager. I see members of my team. I begin to feel a familiar sense of trepidation. The dread associated with saying anything sensible here and the possibility of sitting in silence for the hour. Our consultant is an eminent therapist; kind and thoughtful. The intention here is good but we rarely speak about what matters. I never quite feel safe enough to even begin to say how out of my depth I feel sometimes as a team leader.

It was not as if there was nothing to say. I chose not to and I was not alone. We missed the opportunity to learn but it seemed on balance best to keep it light and stay safe for that hour. The problem was we could never get outside of our training. The process by which we were educated about what things were ok for us to talk about and what was best kept private. In the end I found my self-imposed silence intolerable and eventually left the organisation.

Part of the problem was that our work culture did not contain or endorse the words and concepts to help us put into words what we were feeling and experiencing. We were stuck with our own theories and ideas, which made it hard to think beyond our personal reactions to the work. Sitting in a group like this was unlikely to feel safe enough to talk about our idiosyncratic responses to the work. We were stuck in our personal explanations, aspects of which were silently shared around the group. We missed the opportunity to explore the link between the personal and the wider system, which would have enabled us to talk about the way work was organised. Later, reading the work of Isobel Menzies,[9] Donald Winnicott[10] and more recently Valerie Sinnason[11] and Caroline Elton,[12] the value of having ideas and theories to help explain what is going on can lower the bar and make speaking a bit easier. These legitimatise the shadow side of caring. It can be dirty work, and it can feel wrong to say such a thing out loud. So, best keep quiet.

So, what does this mean in practice? It means we have identified and talked about the ideas and concepts we think will help us name and make sense of the difficult issue that we will face as we work together. We don't wait for the crisis, we anticipate it. Like knowing how to manage and keep safe when the weather turns bad and visibility is lost. While I may feel temporarily confused, I will have the language and concepts to keep safe, keep thinking and manage any panic. I will not compound my situation by not preparing; having an over-developed sense of personal responsibility because we lack good ideas to explain the complexity of our work; or blaming myself (or you) for being incompetent.

Do I care about this issue right now?

If the section above was about wanting to talk if the conditions are right, this section is about not wanting to talk because for the moment, my sense of empathy has slipped away. The people I have worked with, regardless of sector or profession, hold themselves to a high standard. This is a good thing because from it comes exceptional ideas, services and care. There is a downside, which if not addressed, leads to self-silencing.

The COVID-19 pandemic, triggered a re-evaluation of the NHS, social care and those people we took for granted and who made our lives work. We expressed our high regard for these people. At times, in relation to the NHS, as people clapped and put posters in their windows, it crept into something like idealisation. We were scared, so it was important to believe we could be rescued. To be the subject of idealisation, can feel affirming, feel great. It is also to be subject to a subtle pressure to edit one's lived experience. To make it harder to say how one actually feels and to be heard. How one might not be able to care so much; that one is exhausted; had enough for a while. Such ambivalence is normal and can become problematic when suppressed.

The expression of mixed feelings about doing one's job can be silenced in two ways. The first is when managers say to their exhausted teams (often under pressure from above)— *'from Monday, its business as usual'*. This arbitrary cut between crisis and not crisis is just that, arbitrary. It is heard and I think intended (not consciously) to silence people. To not hear or talk about what it is like to work during a crisis; and then have to shift attention to those forced to wait and left untreated. It is a request to keep all that private. Not an opportunity to think about how the system has worked in practice.

The second method is triggered by the first. If I am feeling exhausted, full of mixed feelings and hear the message to keep all that private, I can fall into a sense of shame. Shame is what Jane felt in Chapter 3. She believed she was what was wrong, not her actions, or those of her colleagues. The persistence of her shame and Carole's inability to dislodge it led to Jane being incapacitated professionally and personally. A situation compounded by both Carole and Jane believing that to express ambivalence, talk about her inner life, her thoughts and feelings, was to be taken as further evidence of her unprofessionalism.[13]

If I do not feel safe to talk about not liking aspects of my work, other people, their neediness, their refusal to get better, change their behaviour, the relentless pressure, the pace of the work, then I will keep quiet. Such a decision is rational but a loss. Ambivalence, dislike, hatred are the feelings we experience because we care. To deny this is unkind and suppresses data about the lived experience of people doing the work. When ambivalence is confined to the realm of the personal, to shame it will lead to feeling like an imposter, to burnout.

If I can remain in touch with my ambivalence, I will be less surprised when I (and others) say I do not care. I will not see it as a defining statement but a clue about how I am feeling and what it's like to work around here at the moment. I will take it seriously; something needs to change but not believe I have lost my capacity for kindness. Likewise, when others say things, that in a different context may sound harsh or uncaring, I can hear beyond the words and listen.

Do I know what to say?

I remain surprised by how I can hesitate when faced with the distress of another person. I know I want to say something, should say something, and how I can miss the opportunity. I get caught up in an internal conversation. What should I say; will I sound insensitive; stupid; plain wrong? Reaching out to someone who is traumatised, knowing what to say or do, is hard. It feels like if you get it wrong you will compound their distress. As such, silence can be a natural response. (Of course, if you ask people, most say they would prefer you take the risk than ignore them.)

I can tell myself and I can tell you, this is not the time because there is not the time. No time to gather my thoughts, say something, have a conversation, that work is pressing. This can be an accurate assessment. There is a crisis. We just need to carry on and deal with it all later. It can also be the reason

I give myself and you, to justify my silence, keeping my distance and you quiet. Yes, it's a crisis but does that mean we should not talk?

In the conversation I had with Jane in Chapter 3, I was struck by how quickly harm can be done in the short conversations that characterise organisational life. Just a few minutes can be enough to silence and trigger shame that lasts for months. If this is the case, what good is possible if we only have a few minutes in the midst of a crisis?

Here is an example, not from work, of using time well. It may offer some clues about doing something similar at work.

A long time ago, there was a sudden death in my family. One person stood out, the first person I consciously knew, who did good in the midst of something awful. He was a paramedic. He saw me making a call, to tell my father who was at work, what had happened. He saw me being unable to speak. I was helpless. He reached across, took the phone and said, 'let me'. Two words.

He knew there was nothing he could say that would change what had happened. He knew not to speak, except these two words as events unfolded. What he offered was the sense of being held and contained.[14] Held in the sense he understood that making the call was too much; that it had to be done; and that he needed to intervene. His intervention was containing. He stepped in and changed the situation, by saying 'let me' and then taking the phone, breaking the news.

This paramedic, this stranger, embodied that aspect of silence that is about waiting. Of being in the presence of an event you cannot undo however much you want to. He enabled me to survive this liminal moment, which took me beyond my comprehension. He demonstrated a willingness and capacity to bear witness. A way to let someone know, that you hear them, see them and you can bear to be with them as they struggle. However much they shout and cry. However desperate they feel. You will try and keep them safe and you will not pretend that nothing has really happened or anything much can be undone right now. By this act of embodied silence we let someone know they are important. Not important because they are a brilliant clinician, manager, professional—but because they are a colleague, a fellow being, fellow traveller, entitled to kindness.

If we can hear silence as a means to let someone know they matter, that we will be here, that we are reliable, then silence can be the right thing.[15] As in this example, the paramedic said two words but it was his presence, a steady gaze and posture, in the middle of the madness that was so important. Good clinicians are like this and so are some police officers. They know that forcing people to put things into words, to think, is too much and a way they can avoid just being present. This means, as I think about what is being asked of me, I don't have to worry so much about the words. Maybe just being here, with you now and not allowing myself to be distracted, is the best I can do. It may well be enough to facilitate a recovery. The paramedic did what he did over 40 years ago. I still feel grateful.

Is it safe enough?

All the sections so far are about this question because if I feel safer, I will say more. In this section, I want to consider two aspects of feeling unsafe. The lack of safety that arises from bad leadership, described in Chapter 7, and the lack of safety we can feel when we have something to say that may cause suffering and pain. I will deal with this first.

In Chapter 6, I described the confronting intervention of my supervisor. His refusal to offer the comfort I wanted, which I came to realise was the right thing to have done. He had a duty because of his role, to say difficult things well. It was just unfortunate it was my turn. He could have turned a blind eye and colluded with and reinforced my avoidance. He understood a predicament of speaking up. He could see my vulnerability and realised that is where he needed to go and where I needed to go. His intervention allowed me to turn and face what was really going on, that would not be satisfied with an ersatz fix.

To be this voice of difference is hard, so our silence is understandable. Heffernan[16] writing about wilful blindness invokes Cassandra. Blessed and cursed by prophecy. She can see the truths that are hidden or avoided, doomed to not being heard. 'This is not bullying they're just being clear'; 'I am not upset I am just too sensitive'. We turn a blind eye, deaf ear to what is going on by not inquiring beyond these explanations, partly because we feel we will get no support to do so.

Sinason[17] in her work with people confronted by cognitive, emotional and physical limitations (and the reactions of people around them), argues that it is the work of the therapist to speak to what is unspeakable. It is her phrase to be 'the voice of difference'. To call attention to and then try and make sense of what is painful, present and hidden. The experience of grief is an example.

If we are lucky, we have people who can bear to be with us as we go through the process. People who can tolerate crying, the anger and the withdrawal. People who are there in the first days and still there years later listening and talking. Sinason's work is a reminder that helping someone is a lot about helping them return to thinking. If this is the objective, I have to face a couple of questions of my own. Do I have the skills and know-how to help; is it worth going to where the difficulties are? Or is it preferable to prioritise self-preservation and turn a blind eye?

It is the predicament of the intermediary, the whistle-blower, the constructively awkward to see and hear what is being avoided and to worry if they have the skill and know-how to survive pointing this out. What can make me think 'no thanks' is the sense that the leadership around here is weak, bad, so part of the problem we are not facing.

We can dismiss the possibility of bad leadership in contemporary organisations. We can think leadership is synonymous with 'good'. That the tyrannies of leadership are confined to history. This would be a mistake. Comparisons between political oppression, the willing compliance of professionals in state-sponsored acts and the weekly team meeting, maybe an anathema. However, the role of silence, collusive acquiescence and oppressive behaviours are important to understand in both contexts.[18]

Bad things happen to people when it feels impossible to question; challenge; confront people who do not suffer doubt about their competence; and who refuse the doubt of others. We need to face facts; such people can be effective leaders. They can motivate and align others to a common purpose; they can mobilise the rules and processes to get things done. The kind of people who thrive when aided by a compliant followership and a collusive management team. History tells us, such conditions lead to harm. It is worth keeping in mind that the underlying principles of bad leadership are the same, regardless of context.

Bad leaders get things done by controlling people and aligning them to a shared purpose. They exert control to set limits on what it feels ok to talk about around here. Effective control is achieved when people self-police these limits. Some leaders go a couple of steps further. They seek to control what people think. They close off discussion about the 'good' of the outcome achieved by the common purpose and alignment they have secured.

We are susceptible to the certainty of leaders, including bad ones. Their charm and the meaning they give to our role and our work. They can make us feel special, let us know we belong. They can be a reassuring figure in the middle of uncertainty.[19] They can banish the worry we will be excluded.

The paradoxical price we pay for feeling part of the 'in group' is that our connectedness with others is weakened. It feels less comfortable to have any conversation with our peers that might begin to question what is going on. At this point, we part company with learning. There is nothing to learn, we just need to follow. If this is the case, bad leaders reveal themselves to be frightened of learning. They may have the power to silence but they are also letting us know they are incapable of sustaining an adult relationship. Therefore, we should think hard about offering our agreement.

Adult relationships do consist of loud words, swearing, disagreement, ambivalence and affection. This is the normal state of affairs. If we accept this reality, we may find it easier to talk about how we converse as we work together on a shared task. As Zeldin points out, we have had to learn (and keep re-learning) how to disagree. We have needed to overcome *'the old, ingrained dislike of being interrupted, which seemed like a mutilation'.*[20] Bad managers behave as if they really do suffer this mutilation. An experience that justifies their hostile response. In the face of such leadership, silence makes sense. We know we should speak truth to power and it can feel this is only possible 'in a whisper'.[21]

Judith Butler talks about the power of persistence and presence when facing the 'vexation of social relationships'.[22] Just being there, showing up as the means to express my solidarity with you. To let you know that you matter, that this issue matters. A sense of solidarity to counter the attack on our connectedness. A solidarity and persistence anchored in denial.

It can be useful to think of denial as having two faces.[23] The refusal to face what is in front of us and a stubborn refusal to accept what we are being told. The former is a psychological defence mechanism. The latter is the skill of doubt, expressed in the persistence of another's certainty they are right. It is the insistence that proper language is used.

As Ime expressed in Chapter 4. This is racial discrimination. If you do not face this, then you are not senior leaders who have the best interests of this organisation in mind. You are part of the problem. You have yet to show you are good enough to lead us. As Esther in Chapter 3 points out. The movement of the haematology patient to non-specialist care is dangerous. Not a temporary, administrative move to avoid a breach in the ED.

So, what is possible?

This chapter has been about those times when it does not feel possible to say anything. When we do not have the words; feel too tired or exhausted; worry we will annoy our colleagues and pay for that later; know we are led by people who do not see the value of argument and inter-dependence. If you feel like this, consider the following:

It doesn't have to be perfect

In March 2014 BBC Radio 4[24] set out to celebrate failure. Arguably the world's worst singer, Florence Foster Jenkins was featured. One of the presenters noted dryly that she had freed herself from the need to follow the notes. The singing was magnificent and enthralling in its awfulness; and in freeing herself she was expressing her desire to sing in a way that transcended her obedience to the form. She was freed from the desire to look good.

We can overthink it, assume people are more fragile than they are, that they will not see the good of our intention however clumsy it feels to us. Despite much of what has been written here, mostly our conversations work. We find a way of understanding each other.

Just be there

Silence can be expressed in a turning away; fiddling with my phone or as a steady physical presence. This is silence as the embodiment of kindness. There is **** all I can do right now because this really is an unpleasant situation but I will not compound this by walking away. Being there, attentive, listening, ready, should not be underestimated.

Not staking one's authority on always being right

The situations that are the focus of this book are complex, therefore open to interpretation. What I call bullying, you think of as clarity. Ambiguity about the intentions expressed in our conversations cannot be avoided. It is what makes conversations interesting and creative, if we can bear to be uncertain, disagree and be curious about each other's explanations. If I intervene, I am committing, maybe only for a moment, to my interpretation of what is going on. If I believe I am part of a thinking culture, I am less likely to hesitate, or stay quiet. The stakes are not as high as they can be if speaking into a hostile climate that is often the consequence of poor leadership.

In a thinking culture, my intervention should be taken seriously and not confused with me saying I am right. All I am saying is right now, this is my best thinking about what is going on. While I can claim to know best what I think, I am not claiming this is the only interpretation of the events in front of us. I will have blind spots, defences and lack the language and experience to see it all. However wise I am there will be gaps, something missing in my understanding.

What I ask for, having taken this risk, is a conversation to test, modify or discard this interpretation. It can help to assume that the authority of my role is best exercised in helping to have this sense-making conversation. Not always being the one who knows it all and being right.

And finally forgive yourself

We can judge ourselves a failure when we do not intervene or when we say the wrong thing. This may motivate us, and it can reinforce an unjustified assumption that speaking up, resisting being silenced is an act of individual agency and responsibility. However, to accurately judge ourselves we have to think about the context we find ourselves in. Notice who is present; their role; gender; ethnicity; the time of day; the environment; have we eaten; and the work we are trying to do. All these play a part in deciding to speak and the reception we get when we do.

In the end, speaking up is about creating a pause, to think and review with others. It's a solitary activity expressed in a social context. All the people I have spoken to about this subject are connected by their commitment to break out of the real and self-imposed pressures to stay silent. They are committed to the ethic of argument and diversity of thought. Of trying to keep people safer. They readily speak to their failures and think about how they can improve. What we also need to do is be kind to ourselves. None of us are without sin. In the words of Richard Holloway (2002).[25]

> 'The point I am making here is that we must bring to the examined life a kind of objectivity that enables us to look at ourselves with compassionate impartiality'.
>
> (p. 51)

Notes

1 Naylor, D. (2008) *An investigation into how public sector and community-based practitioners authorise constructively*

awkward intentions. DProf thesis. London: University of Middlesex [Online]. Available from: https://eprints.mdx.ac.uk/6894/ (Accessed: 18th June 2021).

2 Viner, B. (2005) The terribly polite, middle-class war against mobile phones on trains strikes its first blow. *The Independent*, 7th May. Available from: http://comment.independent.co.uk/columnists_m_z/brian_viner/article220395.ece (Accessed: 10th November 2006).

3 Great Britain. Department of Health (2013) *Report of the Mid Staffordshire NHS Foundation Trust Public Inquiry*. London, The Stationary Office. (HC947) Available from: https://www.gov.uk/government/uploads/system/uploads/attachment_data/file/279124/0947.pdf (Accessed: 20th March 2021).

4 Great Britain. Department of Health (2015) *Themes and lessons learnt from NHS investigations into matters relating to Jimmy Savile. Independent report for the Secretary of State for Health February.* Available from: https://assets.publishing.service.gov.uk/government/uploads/system/uploads/attachment_data/file/407209/KL_lessons_learned_report_FINAL.pdf (Accessed: 18th May 2022).

5 Great Britain. Department of Health (2001) *Learning from Bristol: the report of the public inquiry into children's heart surgery at the Bristol Royal Infirmary 1984–1995* Command Paper: CM 5207. Available at: https://webarchive.nationalarchives.gov.uk/ukgwa/20090811143810/http://www.bristol-inquiry.org.uk/final_report/report/index.htm (Accessed: 18th May 2022).

6 Butler, J. (2020) *The force of non-violence*. London: Verso.

7 Butler, J. (2020) *The force of non-violence*. London: Verso.

8 McCaughan, N. and Palmer, B. (1994). *Systems thinking for harassed managers*. London: Karnac.

9 Menzies, L.I. (1988) *Containing anxiety in institutions*. London: Free Association Books.

> 'As our diagnostic work went on, our attention was repeatedly drawn to the high level of tension, distress and anxiety among the nurses. We found it hard to understand how nurses could tolerate so much anxiety and, indeed we found much evidence they could not'
>
> *(p. 45)*.

10 Winnicott, D.W. (1947) Hate in the counter-transference. *International Journal of Psycho-Analysis*, 30, pp. 69–74.
  Winnicott (1947) argues there is an ethical requirement to face one's hatred aroused by 'the heavy emotional burden on those who care' (p. 194). Not to face this emotion is to risk doing awful things.

11 Sinnason, V. (1991) Interpretations that feel horrible to make and a theoretical unicorn. *Journal of Child Psychotherapy*, 17(1), pp. 11–24.

12 Elton, C. (2018) *Also human. The inner lives of doctors*. London: Heineman.

13 A short and helpful article about shame and clinicians is:
  Lyons, B., Gibson, R. and Dolezal, L. (2018) Stories of shame. *The Lancet*, 391(I10130), pp. 1568–1569 [Online]. https://doi.org/10.1016/S0140-6736(18)30897-3 (Accessed: 18th November 2021).

14 Blackwell, D. (1997) Holding, containing and bearing witness: The problem of helpfulness in encounters with torture survivors. *Journal of Social Work Practice*, 11(2), pp. 81–89.

15 Vanstone, W.H. (1982) *The stature of waiting*. London: Darton, Longman and Todd

  'The experience of waiting is the experience of the world as in some sense mattering, as being of some kind of importance'

  (p. 103).

16 Heffernan, M. (2011) *Willful blindness. Why we ignore the obvious to our peril*. London: Simon & Schuster.

17 Sinnason, V. (1992) *Mental handicap and the human condition*. London: Free Association Books.

18 For example, see Adams, G., et al. (2006) Abu Ghraib, administrative evil, and moral inversion: The value of putting cruelty first. *Public Administrative Review*, 66, September/October, pp. 680–693.
  Burleigh, M. (2002) *Death and deliverance. Euthanasia in Germany 1900–1945*. London: Pan.
  Gottlieb, R. (2005) The human material is too weak. In: Roth, J. ed. *Genocide and human rights. A philosophical guide*. Basingstoke: Palgrave.

McKie, A. (2004) 'The demolition of man': Lessons from Holocaust literature for the teaching of nursing ethics. *Nursing Ethics*, 11(2), pp. 138–149.

Roth, J., ed. (2005) *Genocide and human rights. A philosophical guide*. Basingstoke: Palgrave.

Sands, P. (2008) *Torture team. Deception, cruelty and the compromise of law*. London: Allen Lane.

19 See Padilla, A., Hogan, R. and Kaiser, R.B. (2007) The toxic triangle: Destructive leaders, vulnerable followers, and conducive environments. *Leadership Quarterly*, 18, pp. 176–194.

Lipman-Blumen, J. (2005) *The allure of toxic leaders. Why we follow destructive bosses and corrupt politicians—and how to survive them*. Oxford: Oxford University Press.

20 Zeldin, T. (1998) *An intimate history of humanity*. London: Vantage, p. 33,

21 Pawson, R. (2002) Evidence and policy and naming and shaming. *Policy Studies*, 23(3/4), pp. 211–230.

22 Butler, J. (2020) *The force of non-violence*. London: Verso.

23 Cohen, S. (2001) *States of denial. Knowing about atrocities and suffering*. Cambridge: Polity.

> *'Denial in the sense of shutting out the awareness of other's suffering—is the normal state of affairs. This is precisely why so much effort has to be devoted to breaking out of this frame. Far from being pushed into accepting reality, people have to be dragged out of reality'*
>
> *(p. 247).*

24 *The value of failure* (7th March 2014) [radio] BBC Radio 4. 13.45.

25 Holloway, R. (2002) *On forgiveness*. Edinburgh: Canongate.

Index

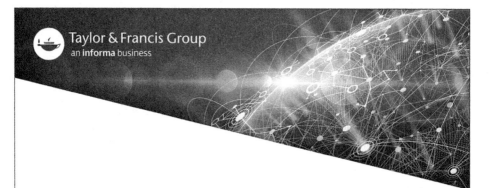

Printed in the United States
by Baker & Taylor Publisher Services